CLAUDE CUÉNOT, son of the famous biologist Lucien Cuénot, studied at the École Normale Superieure and the University of Paris, of which he is a Doctor of Letters. He is Secretary of the Teilhard de Chardin Committee for the publication of Teilhard's works, and a member of the Administrative Council of the Teilhard de Chardin Foundation in Paris. His books include *The Style of Paul Verlaine, Pierre Teilhard de Chardin—A Biographical Study, Lexique Teilhard de Chardin*, etc. He has written numerous articles on aspects of Teilhard's thought.

ROGER GARAUDY is Professor of Philosophy at the University of Poitiers, Director of the Centre for Marxist Study and Research in Paris, and a member of the Political Bureau and of the Central Committee of the French Communist Party. He is the author of: *Théorie Matérialiste de la Connaissance, Les Origines Françaises du Socialisme, l'Église le Communisme et les Chrétiens, Humanisme Marxiste, Karl Marx*, and *Marxisme du Vingtième Siècle*.

Science and Faith in Teilhard de Chardin

This is Volume One in *The Teilhard Study Library*, which examines different aspects of the thought of Teilhard de Chardin and considers its implications for the future of man.

The book is in four parts. The first two are lectures (subsequently expanded for this publication) given by Dr. Cuénot at the first annual conference in October 1966 of The Pierre Teilhard de Chardin Association of Great Britain and Ireland, under the titles: 'The Spirituality of Teilhard de Chardin' and 'Science and Faith in Teilhard de Chardin'. Then follows 'A Comment' which Professor Garaudy made at the conference, thus dramatically throwing into relief the nature of the current dialogue between Christians and Marxists. The book concludes with an original essay by Dr. Cuénot entitled 'Teilhard de Chardin: A Tentative Summing-up', which, taking into account various shades of contemporary opinion, stresses again Teilhard's importance to twentieth-century man.

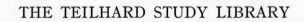
THE TEILHARD STUDY LIBRARY

SCIENCE AND FAITH IN TEILHARD DE CHARDIN

CLAUDE CUÉNOT

with a comment by
ROGER GARAUDY

Translated by
NOËL LINDSAY

GARNSTONE PRESS

91831

First published by
THE GARNSTONE PRESS LIMITED
59 Brompton Road, London S.W.3
in October 1967

SBN: 900391 05 7

Printed by The Anchor Press Ltd., Tiptree, Essex

Contents

Foreword

Teilhard de Chardin never claimed to have constructed a closed and definitive system of thought which would be protected and propagated after his death by 'disciples'. His well-known remark, "If I have had a mission to fulfil, it will only be possible to judge whether I have accomplished it by the extent to which others go beyond me", correctly summarizes the aim and the content of his writings.

To ignore the conditional character of Teilhard's undertaking can only lead to a dogmatism and rigidity of thought which he would have been the first to disown. In an early essay on 'Creative Union' he wrote, "It is very much better to present *tentatively* a mixture of truth and error than to mutilate reality in trying to separate before the proper time the wheat from the chaff. I have followed without hesitation this Gospel rule which is the rule of every intellectual endeavour and of all scientific progress." Again, in THE VISION OF THE PAST, Teilhard insisted that "the views that I present are still, as I said, only at their birth. Do not therefore take them as universally accepted or definitive. What I am putting before you are suggestions rather than affirmations. My principal objective is not to convert you to ideas which are still fluid, but to open horizons for you, to make you think."

Thus Teilhard attempted to sketch the provisional outline of a synthesis which would integrate the Christian Gospel with the evolutionary self-consciousness of modern man—an outline which he hoped others, from many different starting points, would correct, develop and apply.

Consequently, to be faithful to the particular character of Teilhard's achievement requires not simply detailed expositions and clarification of his thought. There are the further essential tasks, critically to determine the areas in which his thought is open to creative development, and to work out in detail the feasibility of its application to the problems which confront and inhibit the growth of human society.

It is our conviction that the interest, ferment and controversy which have surrounded Teilhard's writings since his death in 1955, mark him out not as an ephemeral and modish thinker, but rather as one whose insights and methods can, if explored with discrimination, make a more permanent contribution towards the enrichment, unification and constructive evolution of thought and action in society across existing boundaries of race, politics, religion, science, etc.

Guided by these considerations, the Editors hope that the volumes of *The Teilhard Study Library*[1] will bring such free-ranging and mature reflection upon the implications of Teilhard's *oeuvre* to the notice of a wide public.

General Editors   BERNARD TOWERS

ANTHONY DYSON

---

[1] Details concerning the Association, which is promoting this series of books in association with the publishers, appear on page 110

Introduction

The author scarcely needs an introduction to English readers. Claude Cuénot, son of the famous biologist Lucien Cuénot, is the author of a major biography of Teilhard de Chardin, recently published in an English translation together with a most comprehensive and learned bibliography. He has a detailed and intimate knowledge of Teilhard's writings, both published and unpublished.

In October 1966, The Teilhard de Chardin Association of Great Britain and Ireland held its first major conference under the title 'Evolution, Marxism and Christianity'. Claude Cuénot gave two out of a series of eight lectures that held the close attention of some five hundred people of widely varying beliefs and attitudes. For the purposes of publication he has expanded both those talks, and has contributed a third which he entitles 'A Tentative Summing-up'.

During the discussion that followed one of Dr. Cuénot's spoken addresses, there was a lengthy comment in French from Professor Roger Garaudy, whose own lecture appears in volume 2 in *The Teilhard Study Library*. This comment has been translated, and appears as Part Three in this book. M. Garaudy is Director of the Centre for Marxist Study and Research in Paris, and Professor of Philosophy at the University of Poitiers.

It was a memorable experience to see these two distinguished men, and others, finding common ground for dialogue in the ideas of Teilhard. In planning the publication of the conference proceedings it was thought right that Dr. Cuénot and Professor Garaudy should jointly inaugurate *The Teilhard Study Library*, and that the three contributions by Claude Cuénot should form the major part of the book. The first two volumes together will bring to a far larger audience than could be assembled in a lecture-hall some knowledge and critical appreciation of the thought of a great man of this century, a man whose influence on human affairs is likely to be even greater than that of his nineteenth-century predecessors, Darwin and Marx. In the works of Teilhard de Chardin the evolutionary process is recognized as significant at every level of human experience and human activity. Where there is such comprehension of, and sympathy with, fellow human beings and the natural forces that gave them birth, there also lies the possibility of genuine dialogue, and of an end to destructive warfare, both intellectual and physical.

Jesus College, Cambridge   BERNARD TOWERS
February 1967

PART ONE

The Spirituality of Teilhard de Chardin

by Claude Cuénot

INTRODUCTION

For many years now men have allowed themselves to be influenced by that finely spiritual book, LE MILIEU DIVIN, composed by Teilhard in 1926–27, and which seems clearly destined to take the place of the IMITATION and to be a continuation of the EXERCISES of St. Ignatius. And, if the preaching of LE MILIEU DIVIN in 1928 inspired enthusiasm in Etienne Borne and the young Teacher Training College students of the day, it seems very evident that this work responds particularly to the aspirations of our own rising generation. With your permission I shall adopt a somewhat sinuous and dialectic plan, but it will at least have the advantage of a certain clarity. After briefly describing the needs of young people, I shall show how Teilhard has been able to meet them. I shall then try to recall the traditional elements in his thinking. Finally, in an effort at synthesis, I shall try to bring to light how Teilhard has been able to clothe this traditional thinking of the Church with the most modern spirituality.

I THE ASPIRATIONS OF THE YOUNG

If the spiritual needs of young people could be summed up in a few words, I would speak above all of their *will for effective action*. Whether they are Marxists or not, young people are not content to dream out their lives, they want to mould themselves in moulding the world, to build themselves in building the earth. Their vision of the universe, to use a familiar term, is a praxis. Now, you cannot transform the universe unless you have a certain faith in progress. Young people are forward looking, they live with their eyes on a future which they are not content to look for and guess at, as though it already existed ready made in some container or other, reserved for the possible, but which they wish to build. As Gaston Berger has rightly said: "To turn towards the future instead of looking at the past is not merely to change the spectacle, it is to pass from 'seeing' to 'doing'. The past belongs to the

domain of sentiment; it is made up of all the images whose disappearance we regret and all those we are happy to be rid of. The future, in
contrast, is a matter of will power. To adopt the prospective approach
is to prepare for action."[1]

In other words, for young people, history has a direction, it is made
up of vectors (and therefore oriented), and its apparent confusion,
which seems to turn it into a Brownian movement, conceals the under-
currents. Naturally, in the face of the techniques which are trans-
forming the world and biting on to reality, young people do not remain
inactive; fascinated by technique, they dream of using it to lay their
hands on the springs of the universe.[2] And this faith in progress, this
acute feeling of cosmic responsibility, involves a certain confidence in
the human, and especially in the phenomenon of socialization, that
mass coagulation of human society, for at the same time that young
people are discovering the amplitude and power of cosmic links, they
have discovered the amplitude and power of what can be achieved by
social organization. Young people feel that there *is* something new
under the sun, that mankind has within it dormant forces and un-
worked resources, just as matter, apparently impenetrable, contains
prodigious reserves of energy. Very sensitive to the collective representations which drive youth in upon itself and tend to bring it into conflict
with the family and the older generations, they have the intuition that
social life can be exalting and enriching, even by the very discipline it
imposes. Finally, tormented by a need for inner unity, young people
are very sensitive to antinomies, which leads to a certain heart-rending
and to crises of anguish. They are angry at the resistance of ancient
structures, social, economic, political or intellectual. And, above all,
what chiefly concerns us, they feel a vague uneasiness in the face of a
Christianity which is somewhat mutilating and marginal to the modern
world. We know the ravage wrought by an excessive interpretation of

---

[1] *Prospective*, Paris, Presses Universitaires de France, No. 6, 1960, p. 13.

[2] Cf. Pierre Smulders: "It is a question in the new world, as modern science
reveals it to the eyes of man, of finding God and Christ in everything and
serving the Creator and the Redeemer in the new work on the world which
characterizes our technocratic era". (LA VISION DE TEILHARD DE CHARDIN,
2nd edition, Paris, Desclée de Brouwer, 1965, p. 215. Chapters VIII, IX
and X of this book, which only came to our notice after this talk had
been finalized, provide an interesting analysis of Teilhard's spirituality).

the words of the Gospel, "My kingdom is not of this world"[1] and a
pessimism which turns man into a mere pilgrim and this Earth into a
vale of tears and a place of trial. *Homo viator*. What is the point of
becoming attached, since we must leave it all? We must choose between heaven and earth,[2] and ascesis is primarily an effort of detachment; St. Jerome in his desert and the Stylites at the top of their pillars.
Naturally, the Christian must not be slothful, but the nature, and,
above all, the results of his labours, are unimportant. As Malebranche[3]
says: "*Faith teaches us that all the things of this world are but vanity.*"
We must labour, out of penitence, but the essential thing is not the
result obtained, it is the good intention. In sum: "The great objection
brought against Christianity in our time, and the real source of the
distrust which makes whole blocks of humanity impervious to the
influence of the Church, has nothing to do with historical or theological
difficulties. It is the suspicion that our religion makes its followers
inhuman."[4] "(. . .) Christianity seems lukewarm, and it is marking
time at this moment, because Christians love and admire the Universe
less than pagans; whereas it is they who should be the most completely
human of men."[5]

There is the key word: religion is accused of making "men more

---

[1] These words (John, XVIII, 36) were spoken by Jesus before Pilate to
explain that he was not seeking to raise violent revolution. Jesus in fact
had the idea that to liberate his country, he must first die. But he also
said (Luke, XVII, 21) "(. . .) the Kingdom of God is among you", or, in
other words, without spectacular manifestation, the kingdom is being
achieved here and now, among mankind. Greek scholars will be quick to
see that these divagations on the kingdom are based on a simple misinter-
pretation. Jesus' answer to Pilate means that his kingdom does not *originate*
from this world, but in no way that it is not to be exercised and propagated
in this world.
[2] Cf. the caricatured formula of the philosopher Jean Grenier (who is,
moreover, influenced by the religions of India) : 'We must choose between
the world and God. We can only reach the world through the world and
God through God". (LES ILES, Paris, Gallimard, 1959, p. 135, cited by
J. Onimus, CAMUS, Paris, Desclée de Brouwer, 1965, p. 53.)
[3] RECHERCHE DE LA VÉRITÉ, Ed. du Seuil Vol. IV. Chap 4.
[4] LE MILIEU DIVIN, Paris, Ed. du Seuil, p. 59, English translation, LE
MILIEU DIVIN, Collins, 1960, p. 40.
[5] Parallel passage in NOTE POUR L'ÉVANGÉLISATION DES TEMPS NOUVEAUX
(1919) and in ÉCRITS DU TEMPS DE LA GUERRE (1916–19), Paris, Grasset,
1965, p. 370.

idle, more timid, *less human*".[1] Christianity is regarded as infra-human, as dehumanizing.

As Hegel already said in one of his youthful writings: "Our religion seeks to educate men to be citizens of heaven whose eyes are always turned upwards, and that makes them strangers to human feelings."[2] And the consciences of young people are therefore torn, which leads to anguish and temptation—the temptation to the absurd, since Christian spirituality tends to make the love of earth and the love of Heaven irreconcilable[3] or the temptation to Marxism, since Marxism is primarily a humanism which strives to reconcile man with himself by helping him to overcome his alienations, including religious transcendence, regarded as alienating.

Disgruntled and elderly spirits might object to the young: "We know all about this revolt. It is the classical crisis of originality which brings the rising generation into conflict with the older generations." There is perhaps a little of that, but it is absolutely secondary.[4] In fact, let it be said once and for all, we are changing our age, and young people have an intuition of this, very vague and at the same time very acute. As Teilhard has said, we are passing from a vision in cosmos to a vision in cosmogenesis, from a static universe with cyclical time, to an evolutive universe, which constitutes a single block in movement, which obeys a creative and convergent duration. Two points seem definitely fixed, the primacy of science and the primacy of creative duration. It is science, that sort of natural revelation, which has revealed to us that the universe is in genesis. Man has never been so fully confronted with spatial and temporal dimensions, and it is only today that science has acquired its full powers. The consequence is that our conception of time is singularly enriched. Duration is more than it was thought to be before our days; it is far more interior to beings, or rather, beings

[1] *La Maîtrise du monde et le règne de Dieu* (1916) in ÉCRITS DU TEMPS DE LA GUERRE, Grasset, 1965 p. 83.

[2] HEGELS THEOLOGISCHE JUGENDSCHRIFTEN, ed. Hermann Nohl, Tübingen, 1907, p. 28, cited by R. Garaudy, DIEU EST MORT. ÉTUDE SUR HEGEL. Paris, Presses Universitaires de France, 1962, pp. 20–21.

[3] This is the case of Albert Camus, cf. J. Onimus, CAMUS, pp. 54–55 and passim.

[4] As has been rightly noted by J. Onimus, who speaks with authority on this subject: "It is wrong to say that youth is blasé, cynical and in revolt on principle. It is uneasy." (L'ENSEIGNEMENT DES LETTRES ET LA VIE, Paris, Desclée de Brouwer, 1965, p. 143.)

are far more interior to it. Its role is vaster and more profound than was thought. It has taken on a positive significance. Following this discovery and the progress associated with technology, man has acquired a greater consciousness of his force, of his possibilities, of the value of his action. He now sees that there is a collective job to be done in this world.

II   TEILHARD'S ANSWER

This, then, is the problem to be solved; the spirituality of the IMITATION, however admirable, has been overtaken, because it represents a too mediaeval monastic ideal. How can it be replaced, or, more accurately, completed and filled out? The whole of Teilhard's spirituality, and especially LE MILIEU DIVIN, is addressed to:

(1) Christians whose spirituality is too narrow, who divorce the spiritual too much from the terrestrial, those who have forgotten the Benedictine formula "qui laborat, orat".
(2) believers who hesitate to enter the Church from fear of loving the earth too much.

As Teilhard has said: "Among the two or three natural dogmas which Mankind (. . .) is in the process of conquering, the most categorical and the best loved is undoubtedly that of the infinite value and unplumbed richness of the Universe. Our World bears within itself a mysterious promise of the Future, implicit in its natural Evolution (. . .). If, therefore, I, in the purported name of my Religion, dare to flout such a great hope, which is the idol of my generation, what language must I talk to be understood by nine tenths of my brethren? What sorry figure should I cut beside the doughty fighters for Life, whose rugged endurance (. . .) *invariably ends* in ensuring the triumph of *human* science, *human* power?"[1] "(. . .) I feel the need to prove to myself and to prove to others that the Christian ideal does not make man less 'human' (not only in the sense that it makes him disinterested in certain essential work, but above all in the sense that *it fails to develop in him certain moral forces (preoccupations)* which are unanimously admired today). I think that the unbelievers are mistaken about the value of these new

[1] *La Vie cosmique* (1916) in ÉCRITS DU TEMPS DE LA GUERRE, p. 45.

human virtues, which they set above holiness, or at least that in imagining that they can be cultivated outside religion, they are summoning Mankind to an impossible task. But I also think that we Christians, too, are in great need of 'humanizing' our holiness, in conformity with the rest of our dogmas."

Teilhard's effort to build a new spirituality has a negative aspect and a positive aspect.

The negative aspect first: Teilhard criticizes the idea that the divinization of our effort through the value of the intention can suffice a modern man. He writes, in effect, in LE MILIEU DIVIN: "The divinization of our endeavour by the value of the intention put into it, pours a priceless soul into all our actions; but *it does not confer the hope of resurrection upon their bodies*. Yet that hope is what we need if our joy is to be complete. (. . .) The more I examine myself, the more I discover this psychological truth that no one lifts his finger to do the smallest task unless moved, however obscurely, by the conviction that he is contributing infinitesimally (at least indirectly) to the building of something definitive. (. . .) And that being so, everything which diminishes my explicit faith in the heavenly value of the *results* of my endeavour, diminishes irremediably my power to act."[1]

In other words, LE MILIEU DIVIN proposes a spirituality of human labour, in all its amplitude, in its distant, and even eternal, repercussions, a spirituality which is concerned with the body of the action itself as much as with its spirit (that is to say, the intention). Teilhard goes beyond the idea of work as penitence, without rejecting it. And, constantly, he stresses the value of work: "If Christ is Omega[2] nothing is alien to the physical edification of his universal body (. . .). In the Universe, every movement of material growth is finally for the spirit, and every movement of spiritual growth is finally for Christ. In consequence (. . .) I have the happiness of being able to think that the fruit of my labour is expected by Christ—the fruit, understand well, that is to say, not only the intention of my action, but also the tangible result of my labours, 'Opus ipsum et non tantum operatio'. If this hope is well founded, the Christian must act, and act much, and act with as much seriousness as the most convinced worker for the Earth, in order that Christ[3] may constantly come more and more to birth in

---

[1] Ed. du Seuil, pp. 39, 40 and 41, English translation, pp. 25 and 26.
[2] That is to say, the end of the universe.
[3] Teilhard means the Body of Christ, that is to say, the Mystical Body.

the World around him. More than any unbeliever, he must venerate and promote human effort; effort in all its forms—the human effort, above all, which goes directly to increase the consciousness (that is to say, the being) of Mankind; I mean the scientific research of the truth and the organized pursuit of better social bonds."[1]

And Teilhard adds two clarifications to these exalting prospects. In the first place, not only is God interested in the overall fruit of our work, but he in no way disdains the detail of our terrestrial goals: "No", cries Teilhard, "God does not deflect our gaze prematurely from the work he himself has given us, since he presents himself to us as attainable through that very work. Nor does he blot out, in his intense light, the detail of our earthly aims, since the closeness of our union with him is in fact determined by the exact fulfilment of the least of our tasks."[2] As the great St. Theresa said, "God is among the pots and pans," and as St. Benedict wrote, "The monk must look upon the humblest tools of the monastery as sacred altar vessels."

Secondly, everyone knows that Teilhard was a research worker, geologist and palaeontologist of international standing: it is not surprising that he energetically spurned the false idea that the search for knowledge is evil and forbidden by God. No, in his eyes there is *"an absolute duty of Research"*.[3] As early as 1916, he wrote: "(. . .) *not to search*, not to plumb to the depth the domain of Energies and Thought, not to try to fathom the Real would be a grave *threefold fault*: a *fault of infidelity* towards the Master who has placed Man in the heart of Things to see him consciously and freely prolong their immanent Evolution and his creative work; *a fault of presumption*, which would make them *tempt God*, hoping to gain by indolent prayer, Revelation or Miracle, what could be won by natural work; finally, also, a lack of intellectual integrity . . ."[4] And the month before his death, in March 1955, Teilhard wrote a little work called RECHERCHE, TRAVAIL ET ADORATION.

To sum up in a phrase, I would say, with Teilhard, ". . . the incarn-

[1] *Mon Univers* (1924) in SCIENCE ET CHRIST, Vol. IX of OEUVRES, Paris, Ed. du Seuil, pp. 53–54.
[2] LE MILIEU DIVIN, Ed. du Seuil, pp. 53–54, English translation, p. 36.
[3] *Le Prêtre* (1918) in ÉCRITS DU TEMPS DE LA GUERRE, p. 299.
[4] *La Maîtrise du monde et le règne de Dieu* (1916) in ÉCRITS DU TEMPS DE LA GUERRE, p. 81–82. Parallel passage in the letter of 4 August 1916, in GENÈSE D'UNE PENSÉE, LETTRES 1914–1919, Paris, Grasset, 1961, p. 148. English translation, THE MAKING OF A MIND, London, Collins, 1965, p. 116.

ate God did not come to diminish in us the glorious responsibility and splendid ambition that is ours; of *fashioning our own self*."[1]

In this communion with God through action, the Christian virtues are, of course, preserved, but find themselves renewed and made more dynamic. The true charity is not the barren fear of doing evil, but the determination to force, all together, the gates of Life. True purity is not a bloodless separation from things, but a drive through every beauty. No, purity does not lie in separation, but in a deeper pene-tration of the Universe. As Teilhard says in LE MILIEU DIVIN: "Purity, in the wide sense of the word, is not merely abstaining from wrong (that is only a negative aspect of purity), nor even chastity (which is only a remarkable special instance of it). It is the rectitude and the impulse introduced into our lives by the love of God sought in and above everything. He is spiritually impure who, lingering in pleasure or shut up in selfishness, introduces, within himself and around himself, a principle of slowing-down and division in the unification of the universe in God. (. . .) Thus understood, the purity of beings is measured by the degree of the attraction that draws them towards the divine centre, or, what comes to the same thing, by their proximity to the centre."[2] In other words: "*The specific action of purity* (. . .) *is* (. . .) *to unify the internal powers of the soul* in the act of a unique passion, extraordinarily rich and intense. The pure soul, finally, is the one which, surmounting the multiple and disorganizing attraction of things, tempers its unity (that is to say, matures its spirituality) in the ardours of the divine simplicity."[3] Conversely, impurity, in all its forms, is the relapse into the Many.

Another example of virtue rethought by Teilhard is resignation. Christian resignation is sincerely considered and blamed by many honest people as one of the most dangerously narcotic elements of the "opium of religion". Teilhard answers in these fine words: "We are only entitled to resign ourselves to evil when we have first resisted it up to the limit of our strength. *We must therefore take great pains to succeed in submitting ourselves to the will of God.* God is not indifferently everywhere in the interferences and passivities of life, but only at *the point of balance* between our strenuous efforts to grow and the resistance

---

[1] LE MILIEU DIVIN, Ed. du Seuil, p. 62. English translation, p. 43.
[2] LE MILIEU DIVIN, Ed. du Seuil, pp. 165–166. English translation, p. 124.
[3] *La Lutte contre la multitude* (1917) in ÉCRITS DU TEMPS DE LA GUERRE, p. 126.

of the external to our domination."[1] In other words, resignation is only to be found at the peak of effort. We are a long way from the musings of Tolstoy on non-resistance to evil, we are a long way from the ahimsa, the non-violence of Gandhi, we are a long way from that caricature of Christianity which inspired the sarcasms of Nietzsche on the sweet little gentleness of the sheeplike Christians.[2] The Christian option should therefore be presented as a choice, not precisely between heaven and earth, but between two efforts to achieve the Universe *intra* or *extra Christum*, internally or externally to Christ.

III TEILHARD AND TRADITION

I sum up all that has gone before: "Normally, the soul which desires to belong solidly to Christ must prepare within itself, as the foundation of its celestial perfection, abundant material to be sanctified, *a rich nature*. Science, art, industry, social activity . . . all that is necessary to offer worthy material to the influence of Jesus. Nothing of this should be alien to the Christian, *inasmuch as* he is a Christian. The first duty, individual and apostolic, of the supernaturalized man is therefore to elaborate in himself, for Christ, by the use of his creatures, a vigorous *ego*. His first care, *similar* (but in appearance only) to that of the pagan, must be to prolong, by human effort, in all the directions which lead to the spirit, the still unfinished work of visible creation."[3] Transcendence has ceased to dispossess man and to tear him, it no longer prevents him from being at home in the world. What is given to man is not taken away from God. As Father Chenu has said, "The more man is man, the more chance God has of being God."

[1] *Mon Univers* (1924) in science et christ, Ed. du Seuil, Vol. ix, p. 101.
[2] On the dynamic force of Teilhard's charity, cf. *Super-humanité, Super-Christ, Super-Charité* (1943) in science et christ, Ed. du Seuil, pp. 213–214.
[3] *Forma Christi* (1918) in écrits du temps de la guerre, p. 345; cf. Dietrich Bonhoeffer, "Religious people speak of God when human perception is (often just from laziness) at an end, or human resources fail: (. . .) always, that is to say, helping our human weakness or on the borders of human existence. (. . .) I should like to speak of God not on the borders of life but at its centre, not in weakness but in strength, not, therefore, in man's suffering and death but in his life and prosperity", letters and papers from prison, 2nd ed., London, 1956, p. 124. Cited in R. Garaudy, marxisme du 20e siècle, Paris and Geneva, 1966; la Palatine, p. 175f.

This spirituality may possibly give you an ambivalent impression. It seems to meet very exactly the aspirations of the rising generation. But what are its theological bases and what relation does it bear to tradition?

Let us try to start by explaining the theological foundations.

(1) At the root of this spirituality—and this is why it is modern—we find a certain concept of divine creation. It has no room for the over-simplified idea of a creator God who, in the beginning, created the cosmos once and for all, and, as it were extrinsically, like a potter shaping a vessel of clay. His creative effort is immanent in the world, and the act by which he maintains it in being is identical with the creative act. Even more, the evolution of the world, which Teilhard calls cosmogenesis, should be regarded as a natural dimension of God's creative action. Thus "we may perhaps imagine that creation finished a long time ago. This is a mistake, it is continuing more than ever and in the loftiest zones of the World (. . .). And we serve to complete it, even by the humblest work of our hands".—"Become, by existence, the conscious collaborators of a Creation which is continuing in us (. . .), we must aid God with all our strength and handle matter as though our salvation depended solely on our industry."[1] In other words, in an infinitesimal, but perfectly real, fashion, we are summoned to the dignity of co-creators in the setting of a "creatio continua".

(2) Grace, supernatural charity, though a free gift of the divine loving kindness, is not something extrinsic to the world, which falls from heaven, we know not where or how. It needs a natural food: "Because he desired to rise too fast and too far, man has perhaps felt a weakening of those energies which he wanted to concentrate too exclusively on Heaven. God has not thought fit to create in us, in order that we may love Him, a new and distinct focus of affection. Following the particular order of our World, where *everything is made by the transfiguration of a pre-existing analog*, it certainly seems that divine Charity in its origins in us is nothing but the supernaturalized and purified flame which burns in the face of the promises of the Earth."[2]—Grace does not destroy, but it consumes. As Teilhard has written, addressing himself to God: "I perceive (. . .) that all perfection, even natural perfection, is

[1] *Science et Christ* (1921) in the volume of the same name, Ed. du Seuil, p. 58.
[2] *La Maîtrise du monde et le règne de Dieu* (1916) in ÉCRITS DU TEMPS DE LA GUERRE, pp. 75–76.

the necessary basis of the mystical and ultimate organism which you are constructing in the midst of all things. You do not destroy the creatures which you have adopted, Lord, but you transform them by consuming all the good that centuries of creation have elaborated in them."[1]

This is certainly the classical Thomist formula "gratia non tollit naturam, sed perficit". If Teilhard's Pantokrator shines with all the metaphysical splendours of the Neo-Logos, of Christ universal and Christ-Omega, it is because he is a fundamentally incarnate Christ. In Teilhard, as in the Bible, and perhaps even more in the Greek Fathers, the links between soteriology and cosmology are revealed as indissoluble.[2] In Teilhard, as in the Bible, cosmic concepts are never abstract, but remain essentially linked to soteriological concepts and appear as their universal consequence. It follows that in Teilhard as in the Bible, all the cosmic-universal properties of Christ (including his pre-existence) operate only by virtue of his incarnation.[3] If, therefore, Teilhard (who, by his physical sense of the incarnation, manifests a radical hostility to docetism) envisages all creation as a "theatrum gloriae Dei"[4] who can be surprised to hear him, too, chant a "canticle of creatures"?

(3) The last root: This spirituality of Teilhard's is a spirituality of the resurrection, and therefore very close to the Christianity of the Greek Fathers.[5] As early as 1916, Teilhard wrote: "(. . .) from that mysterious Whole which is Matter, something must pass, through the Resurrection, into the world of the heavens—my efforts for human progress being even (?? perhaps) the necessary condition for the elaboration of the new Earth"[6]—"(. . .) everything which mankind produces, in every

---

[1] LE PRÊTRE (1918), ÉCRITS DU TEMPS DE LA GUERRE, p. 298.

[2] Cf. *La Vie cosmique* (1916) ibid, p. 49: "By the Incarnation, which has saved men, the whole Destiny of the Universe has been transformed and sanctified."

[3] We have merely taken these ideas from Pastor A. Szekeres, of the Netherlands, who is to develop them in a CRITIQUE OF THEOLOGICAL REASON. The whole credit for this realization goes to him.

[4] Expression borrowed from Calvin.

[5] It has been said that Teilhard's project could be described as a 'theology of glory' (F. Refoulé, TEILHARD DE CHARDIN ET BULTMANN, *Parole et Mission*, 15 October 1964, p. 602).

[6] Letter of 15 March 1916 to Father Victor Fontoynont, in H. de Lubac, LA PENSÉE RELIGIEUSE DU PÈRE PIERRE TEILHARD DE CHARDIN, Paris, Aubier, Ed. Montaigne, 1962, p. 350.

order, of real and transmissible value, constitutes, as it were, a blossoming forth of its being, a prolongation or a perfecting of its organism, a vast collective body, destined for resurrection no less than each of our individual bodies." St. Ambrose already exclaimed: "Resurrexit in eo mundus, resurrexit in eo coelum, resurrexit in eo terra!"[1] Just as redemption was cosmic, so resurrection will be cosmic, embracing the universe and man and mankind taken collectively. Only the grace of God makes divine, but man, in the least of his acts, can create something which is capable of being made divine, when he acts consciously or unconsciously under the sign of God. As Teilhard has very well said in a spiritual notebook "I have always acted as if the flower of the World could lead to the flower of Heaven".[2]

This view is confirmed by His Eminence Cardinal Feltin: "The final blaze will not be purely destructive: it will transfigure and convey into the Divine glory, after purifying it, everything which in this world has been revealed, by the work of the Creator and the labour of man as beautiful, true and worthy of God. Labour is therefore, in this exalting perspective for man, the direct preparation of that which God will transfigure at the last day. The work which issues from the hands of man will not be purely frail and transitory, doomed to destruction, but, mysteriously, something of it will subsist to all eternity."[3]

The theological and biblical bases of this spirituality are therefore more than reassuring. It would be easy to demonstrate that Teilhard is directly in the Jesuit tradition of the *Spiritual Exercises* of St. Ignatius Loyola, and exercises himself to see God present and acting in all things, in all beings. Perhaps he even knew the book of Cardinal Bellarmine (a Jesuit!) *The ascent of the mind to God by the ladder of his creatures.*[4] More generally, it may be recalled that Christian humanism, with Erasmus and St. Francis of Sales, is contemporary with the humanist

[1] The world is resurrected in him, heaven is resurrected in him, the earth is resurrected in him.

[2] Cited by Louis Barjon, S.J., in LE GOÛT DU RÉEL. TEILHARD DE CHARDIN. *Vie enseignante. Notre temps.* (Paris) No. 183, March-April 1966, p. 16, col. 1.

[3] *Le Travail et la condition humaine*, November 1962, in LA DOCUMENTATION CATHOLIQUE, Paris, 17 February 1963, 45th year, Vol. LX, no. 1394, p. 246, col. 2.

[4] The Latin title is *De ascensione mentis ad Deum per scalas creaturarum.* The beginning of p. 125 of LE MILIEU DIVIN, Ed. du Seuil, seems to paraphrase this title. English translation, Collins, London, p. 92

Renaissance.[1] But a peevish spirit might still find objections. Does Teilhard, on the model of Lamennais, confound the transformation of society with the establishment of the Kingdom of God? Is he a sort of activist tainted with the malady of temporalism? In a word, is this naturalism with semi-pelagianism on the horizon?

This would be a singular misunderstanding of Teilhard, who fore-stalled the objection. As early as 1918, he wrote: "(. . .) twofold danger: (1) aggrandizing the Universe to the extent of eclipsing or 'materializing' God—(2) making use of the natural resources and affections of life to the extent of profiting from them and enjoying them like a pagan."[2] In a letter of capital importance of 12 December 1919, he told his friend and confidant, Father Auguste Valensin: "I admit *fundamentally* that the achievement of the World is only consummated through a death, a "night", a turning back, an excentration and a quasi-depersonalization of monads.[3] The aggregation of a monad in Christ presupposes a sort of internal disaggregation in it, that is to say a rearrangement of its whole being, the condition of its re-creation and integration in the Pleroma (. . .). Note this well: I attach no final and absolute value to the various human constructions. I think that they will disappear, recast in something wholly new and unimaginable. (. . .) What I love in them is not their particular form, but their func-tion, which is to construct mysteriously, first something which can be made divine,—and then, by the grace of Christ placed upon our effort, something divine."[4]

It should be clearly understood that what we have just described was only the first phase of an ascetic work, that of a certain attach-ment to the world, of a certain immersion in the Universe. But there

---

[1] St. Augustine, Pascal and Kierkegaard (with Albert Camus as a distant epigonos) are ranged against this Christian humanism; for them (very broadly speaking) it is impossible to arrive at God *through* the world, by trying to spiritualize the temporal. This is a tragic Christianity, of rupture and dissociation. The rupture is also there in Teilhard, but it remains primarily eschatological. Naturally, here and now, the Christian experiences a process of excentration, but this process is simultaneous with that of centration.

[2] *Mon Univers* (1918) in ÉCRITS DU TEMPS DE LA GUERRE, p. 346.

[3] *i.e.* persons.

[4] This letter was written at a time when Teilhard and Blondel were in correspondence through the channel of Valensin. But this particular in no way detracts from the force of the text. On the intellectual and spiritual planes, Teilhard was specially incapable of a false complaisance.

is a second phase in the formation of the soul, that of detachment or emersion from the World, and as Teilhard says, "it is the hour of the *specifically Christian* operation, in which Christ, preserving in man the treasures of his nature, voids him of his egoism and takes his heart— a dolorous hour for the lower nature, delivered up to the *diminishing forces* of this World, but an hour of delight for the man enlightened by Faith, who feels himself evicted from himself and dying, by the force of a Communion."[1] After centration upon oneself, it is excentration "in which there founders for a time, not only the success of individuals, but the whole appearance of any human advantage (. . .) the tearing phase of a diminution which nothing tangible comes to compensate".[2]

I will not dwell on this theme, which goes beyond my subject. I will content myself with referring you to the passages in LE MILIEU DIVIN devoted to the passivities of diminishment and death, and I sum up this third part in a sentence: "(. . .) LE MILIEU DIVIN paints the picture of the Christian of all times in the situation of today."[3]

IV   TEILHARD'S SYNTHESIS

Traditional thinkers, who are not always wrong, may therefore feel a certain reassurance. We have both ends of the chain in our hands; Teilhard, while following the eternal lesson of the Church, has known how to feel passionately with his own time. But there is still a snag. It is all very well to hold both ends of the chain, but is it enough for a mind hungry for synthesis? Now Teilhard was a man of synthesis.

Here we come to the perspectives which I believe to be the most powerful and the most able to confer inner peace on a man of the twentieth century. I sum them up in two formulas which I will go on to expand.

Effort is crucifying.

[1] *Forma Christi* (1918) in ÉCRITS DU TEMPS DE LA GUERRE, p. 346.
[2] It would be a real mistake to attribute a purely temporal value to this word "phase". It is rather a dialectical moment. "Centration" and "excentration" soon reveal themselves to be practically simultaneous. It is the same thing as in the case of "reflection" and "co-reflection" on the phenomenological and epistemological plane; the individual threshold of reflection is already, inchoately, co-reflection.
[3] This fine phrase comes from Father H. de Lubac in DU BON USAGE DU MILIEU DIVIN (unpublished).

Human effort is a gift commenced.

1. "Nothing is more crucifying than effort, and than spiritual effort (. . .). Each individual existence, faithfully led, is strewn with the husks abandoned by our successive metamorphoses—and the whole Universe leaves behind it a long series of states in which it would perhaps have liked to take its pleasure, but from which the pitiless necessity of growth has constantly snatched it."[1]

2. Human effort is a gift commenced: "Under the spur which thus urges him on unceasingly to escape from himself to arrive at the term of himself, that is to say, at the Term of the World, the Man who faithfully follows the naturally rising slope of the Universe is less and less interested in his individual success (as an individual). But, after desiring to perfect himself for himself, he is gradually attracted by the higher realities, vaster, more lasting, nearer to the absolute than his personal reality. (. . .) By virtue of the structure of the World (that is to say its universal convergence on Christ) the man who acts religiously ends by thinking almost no more of himself; (. . .) he tends, by an inescapable drive, to be no longer interested in anything but the progress of the soul."[2] "The sincere and faithful artificer of Progress (. . .) has made *a great and perpetual renunciation*. He works, he forgets himself, he detaches himself, even, since he loves causes more than himself, and he seeks the success of human life more than his selfish and personal success."[3]

This, then, is the living logic of action, that we can conquer ourselves and grow only by dying gradually to ourselves. To act worthily and usefully is to unite. But to unite is to transform oneself into something greater than oneself. "From the point of view of Incarnation, understood in a wide sense, detachment and renunciation become above all the act of not looking so much for things, but looking in everything for what is greater than it and beyond it—which makes it possible to love things without remaining in them, which makes it possible to overpass them, while taking them with one."[4]

Nicole had already said, in a Jansenist context of despising the

---

[1] *Mon Univers* (1924) in SCIENCE ET CHRIST, Ed. du Seuil, Vol. IX p. 98.
[2] *Mon Univers* (1924), ibid, pp. 98–99.
[3] *La Maîtrise du monde et le règne de Dieu* (1916) in ÉCRITS DU TEMPS DE LA GUERRE, p. 82.
[4] *Essai d'intégration de l'homme dans l'univers*, 4th talk, 10 December 1930, pp. 18–19 of the typewritten original.

world, which is not at all that of Teilhard: "The laborious life always diminishes the love of the world, the love of Life, the attachment to temporal things."[1] This is the very same idea; the man who works is a great renouncer. But Teilhard is radically opposed to Nicole in refusing to identify detachment and indifference.

CONCLUSION

In conclusion, Teilhard has, if not discovered, at least lived and formulated:

(1) a new type of ascesis,

(2) a new type of holiness.

1. He has discovered, at the cost of very stern effort, ascesis by overtaking, detachment by traversing: "Like the jet of flame that effortlessly pierces the hardest metal, so the spirit drawn to God penetrates through the world, and makes its way enveloped in the luminous vapours of what it sublimates with Him. It does not destroy things, nor distort them; but it liberates things, directs them, transfigures them, animates them. It does not leave things behind, but, as it rises, it leans on them for support; and carries along with it the chosen part of things."[2]

"The Christian was for a long time able to pass as a man who professed disdain for what happened. Very well, what he should henceforth be recognized by is a peerless devotion of all his being to the creative power that has built the world 'usque adhuc' and up to its material and sensible spheres; his true character must be *an exceptional fervour for Creation*. Formerly, to detach oneself from the World could mean leaving the World. In future this word must mean to traverse the World (. . .)."[3]

2. He has discovered, and partly lived, a new type of holiness, the general sanctification of human effort: "What, then, in the end, will be the *ideal Christian*, the Christian both old and new, who WILL RESOLVE, IN HIS SOUL, THE PROBLEM OF VITAL EQUILIBRIUM by making

[1] Quoted by B. Groethuysen, ORIGINES DE L'ESPRIT BOURGEOIS EN FRANCE, 4th edition, Paris, Gallimard, p. 215, Bibliothèque des Idées.

[2] LE MILIEU DIVIN, Ed. du Seuil, p. 177. English translation, Collins p. 132.

[3] LE SENS HUMAIN (1929), p. 9 of the Marcel Legaut typescript (to appear in Vol. XI of the OEUVRES, Ed. du Seuil).

ALL THE SAP OF THE WORLD flow into HIS STRIVING AFTER THE DIVINE
TRINITY? . . ."[1]

"For what is sanctity in a creature if not to adhere to God with
the maximum of his strength?—and what does that maximum adherence
to God mean if not the fulfilment—in the world organized around
Christ—of the exact function, be it lowly or eminent, to which that
creature is destined both by natural endowment and by supernatural
gift?

"Within the Church we observe all sorts of groups whose members
are vowed to the perfect practice of this or that particular virtue:
mercy, detachment, the splendour of the liturgy, the missions, contem-
plation. Why should there not be men vowed to the task of exemplifying,
by their lives, the general sanctification of human endeavour?—men
whose common religious ideal would be to give a full and conscious
explanation of the divine possibilities or demands which any worldly
occupation implies?"[2]

I do not know that Teilhard ever read Rimbaud, but LE MILIEU
DIVIN seems to me to be the most shattering answer which the Church
has been able to find to that desperate cry of the young seer which
resounds through *Les Premières Communions*:

"Christ! O Christ, éternel voleur des énergies!"[3]

*Printed with acknowledgements to Editions du Seuil, Paris, for permission
to include this contribution.*

[1] *La Maîtrise du monde et le règne de Dieu* (1916) in ÉCRITS DU TEMPS DE LA
GUERRE, p. 81.
[2] LE MILIEU DIVIN, Ed. du Seuil, p. 57. English translation, Collins, p. 39.
[3] "Christ! O Christ, eternal theif of energies!"

PART TWO

Science and Faith in Teilhard de Chardin

by Claude Cuénot

Science and faith. . . . A burning topic of the day.[1] It was the Renaissance which first began to dwell upon it insistently. In the ancient world Christianity had in practice purely and simply adopted the cosmology of the day, with its geocentrism and its hierarchy of interlocking spheres, and it preserved this cosmology in the Middle Ages, being content to baptise it. But the sixteenth century, the age of dissociation, shattered this harmony by making two fundamental discoveries: first, of many unknown lands peopled by men who knew not Christ, and secondly of heliocentrism, the contribution of Copernicus. Even in the sixteenth century "natural philosophers" like Giordano Bruno were already at odds with religion, but it was the seventeenth century which witnessed the first serious clashes between the two spiritual forces, science and faith: Galileo, embracing heliocentrism, was condemned by the Inquisition[2] and scientific research in the

[1] The great Protestant philosopher, Georges Gusdorf, has devoted a brilliant work to it, SCIENCE ET FOI AU MILIEU DU XXe SIÈCLE, which is in its second edition (Paris, Société Centrale d'Evangélisation, s.d.). "Science and Faith" was the subject of an exhibition arranged at Vincennes in 1962 by Abbé Le Corvec. Fayard, the publishers, brought out a collection, SCIENCE ET FOI, in the same year, including, inter alia, an article by Father François Russo, S.J., whose title speaks volumes, Cent années d'un dialogue difficile entre la Science et la Foi (1850–1950). Jean-Marie Aubert, in his work RECHERCHE SCIENTIFIQUE ET FOI CHRÉTIENNE, Paris, Fayard, Collection "Jalons", has devoted a chapter to Teilhard, under the title, Un exemple d'unité: Teilhard de Chardin (Chap. VI, pp. 114–122). Valuable particulars are to be found in Georges Crespy, DE LA SCIENCE À LA THÉOLOGIE; ESSAI SUR TEILHARD DE CHARDIN, Neuchâtel, Delachaux et Niestlé, Cahiers théologiques 54 (cf. Chap. I. L'évolution et ses problèmes, pp. 7–24 and VIII, La théologie après Teilhard, pp. 113–124). Cf. also F. Russo, SCIENCE ET FOI, Paris, Desclée de Brouwer, 1966, p. 35–48, Recherches et débats, No. 54. There is in Fribourg (Switzerland) an International Institute for synthesis between science and faith.
[2] He was not to be removed from the Index until 1822, a century after Newton; although Paul VI at Florence called him "a great Christian"; and his rehabilitation proceedings are still awaited.

C

Catholic countries, except France, was largely stifled for several centuries. Happily, in France, with its principle of the liberty of the Gallican Church, the situation was a little different. Pascal is a great scientist, Descartes is prudent enough not to embroil himself with the Church, the Jesuits become Cartesians, and the Sorbonne, the citadel of reaction and obscurantism, cannot inhibit the progress of science.

In the eighteenth century, however, the scientific movement in France escapes almost completely from the Church, which condemns the "philosophes" and the Encyclopaedists, the heirs of the "libertins" of the seventeenth century, themselves the children of the Renaissance. In the nineteenth century, notwithstanding the existence of great Catholic (or spiritually-minded) scientists, science, become triumphant, henceforth asserts the claim to take the place of religion. We then flounder in the midst of ambiguities: evolutionism, for example, being amalgamated with materialism. In the twentieth century, the Church endeavours to climb back again. Catholic scientists multiply and gain as much honour as the non-catholics. No doubt, apart from Pierre Termier and a few other militants, they remain in watertight compartments, religion on one side, faith on the other. But, as Teilhard notes: "(. . .) Christianity has done a great deal to adjust its physical and philosophical background to the legitimate demands of science."[1] Scientism, for its part, moderates its claims. As Teilhard also notes: "(. . .) it has become clear to the outstanding modern scientists and thinkers that human progress cannot continue on its way without developing its own mystique, a mystique founded on *faith* in the value and infallibility of evolution."[1]

This, very broadly, was the situation when Teilhard, in the first ten years of the twentieth century, became alive to science, and more specifically to geology, palaeontology and prehistory, with very large extensions into biology and ethnology, and views on contemporary physics and astronomy.

Teilhard presents a phenomenon almost unique in this first half-century, which gives his experience its great value as an example. In this first part of our survey, we shall content ourselves with a first approximation and we shall take the line (highly artificial as it is) of dealing in

[1] HISTORY OF THE CONFLICT BETWEEN RELIGION AND SCIENCE, Peking 1944 (No. 406 of the Cuénot bibliography).

turn, without cross-reference, with the mystic and the scientist.

It is still not sufficiently well known that Teilhard was an authentic mystic, living habitually in "the expectation and sentiment of a great Presence", capable, even in the conduct of scientific research, of experiencing "a nameless beatitude" in recalling that he possessed "in a total, incorruptible and loving Element, the supreme Principle in which everything subsists and is animated".[1] What still misleads the public is first, that a great many of the most overwhelming texts are still unpublished, as the religious works are to form the last part of the published *works*, but mainly the fact that some people, unaware of recent work on mysticism, still think that it must be accompanied by praeternatural phenomena, such as visions, ecstasies and the like. This is a serious mistake. Such accompaniments to the mystical life are evidence, not of a privilege accorded by God, but simply of human weakness, ill able to bear the presence of the supernatural. In other words, they are epiphenomena.[2]

We might try to characterize Teilhard's mysticism. The first thing that strikes us is its astonishing precocity. From the age of reason, about seven, the need for the absolute remains constantly present in the child, without ever being eclipsed. Born into a fundamentally pious family, brought up by an admirable mother,[3] he very soon began to love Jesus and he was taught a very special devotion to the Sacred Heart, which was to last all his life in an original form, the Heart of Jesus becoming the symbol of the Christic energy which transverberates the universe. It was his mother, too, who taught him that "the whole effort of 'evolution' can be reduced to the justification and development of a love (of God)"[4] and that, in consequence, the history of the world is the act of God.

Teilhard, like all mystics, nurses a very keen sense of the transcendence of God. He is well aware that the world will die and that we cannot say with certainty what parts of it will survive, though the flower of human contribution cannot perish. He even goes so far as to

[1] Letter to Léontine Zanta of 15 October 1926 in Pierre Teilhard de Chardin, LETTRES À LÉONTINE ZANTA, Paris, Desclée de Brouwer, 1965, p. 79.
[2] Nevertheless, it seems that Teilhard, before the battle of Verdun, enjoyed some kind of mystical favour, as described in the first of the CONTES COMME BENSON.
[3] She was called "the Saint".
[4] Letter of 15 August 1936.

say that the universe could be annihilated without the blaze of un-created rays diminishing or God being touched in his essence. But Teilhard nevertheless remains a cosmomystic. His fundamental mystical intuition is the Christic diaphany of matter, or in other words, at the cost of a very long and very hard ascesis, he has succeeded in deciphering and perceiving the divine countenance of Christ as a sort of watermark in matter, and all the stages of his inner life, the purple of matter, the gold of the spirit, the white incandescence of the "Personal", constitute the milestones of a progress in the transfiguration of matter by Christ, or, more accurately, by Christic energy, irradiated by the Heart of Jesus.

One could apply to Teilhard what has been written of the apostle John by Father Paul de la Croix, o.c.d.: "John was profoundly possessed by the two complementary aspects of the unique Reality; the trans-cendence and the immanence of God. This transcendence and this immanence, presented and acting in the Word made flesh, enveloped, impregnated, penetrated him (...). In the upspringing of the Word in the bosom of God, his Work mounts; there is no other work but his and it has no sense or purpose but in him (...). Neverthe-less, this work, though distinct from God, is not external to him. He bears it within himself (...). If the terms of transcendence and imman-ence can be applied conjointly to God, it is because God is not an 'ob-ject'. He is the unit of the Many which he creates (...). In him (...) each thing knows a communion with all the others, because nothing exists which does not, in him, participate in everything which is."[1]

The diaphany which Teilhard perceived was *the reality* of the immanence of the Word, *everything in all* creatures, by the effect of evolutive Creation, original upspringing, Incarnation, Eucharistiza-tion[2] up to the consummation in the One. Hence arises a permanent intuition of the presence of Christ which made witnesses say that Teilhard saw, as it were, in transparency, through things and people. Even when he was examining a stone—he had singularly keen sight —he seemed to see beyond it, so that this man, so near by his warm

---

[1] L'ÉVANGILE DE JEAN, Paris, Desclée de Brouwer.

[2] The process by which Christ, present and acting through the consecrated Host, progressively assimilates to himself mankind, and, through mankind, the universe, indispensable to complete the plenitude of the Mystical Body of Christ. Instead of this term, Teilhard uses the expression "Sacra-ment of the world".

sympathy, by his sense of friendship, by his sensitivity, at the same time remained desperately remote.

In the sequel, there is nothing astonishing in the fact that this cosmomystic practised an ascesis, not of separation but of the traversing of creatures, a difficult and even dangerous ascesis for anyone who does not experience a sufficient love of God, but which Teilhard succeeded in practising and perfecting since, in him, this love commanded his desires and his will to such an extent that he very soon reached the state in which prudence could be defined as "burning with a stronger flame". Creatures, in a movement of perpetual overpassing, seemed to him to be a ladder leading straight to God. This is, in truth, an ascesis, since each time it is a rejection of repose, it is uprooting, departure for a loftier summit. In the *Mass on the World*,[1] Teilhard says to God: "First of all I shall stretch out my hand unhesitatingly towards the fiery bread which you set before me. This bread, in which you have planted the seed of all that is to develop in the future, I recognize as containing the source and the secret of that destiny you have chosen for me. To take it is, I know, to surrender myself to forces which will tear me away painfully from myself in order to drive me into danger, into laborious undertakings, into a constant renewal of ideas, into an austere detachment where my affections are concerned."

It is true that when Teilhard, in LE MILIEU DIVIN, describes the unitive way, it is not difficult, especially after re-reading LE MILIEU MYSTIQUE, to divine that he speaks from the fullness of his own knowledge. It is true that he confided to Father Pierre Leroy, on 26 December 1954, "I can assure you that now I live in the constant presence of God".[2] But Teilhard did not disregard the Cross. Did he not compare evolution to the Stations of the Cross? Only, when he contemplated the Cross he did not see only the infamous wood, he also contemplated the God upon it. For Teilhard, as for Greek spirituality, Christ is first and foremost the glorious Christ of the resurrection and the Parousia, he is Christ Pantokrator, the cosmic Christ, master of all things—the history of mankind coming down to an education of men by God. This is the explanation of the twofold character of Teilhard's piety, the perpetual offering of the cosmos to God—think of LA MESSE SUR LE MONDE—and

---

[1] HYMNE DE L'UNIVERS, Editions du Seuil, p. 29. English translation, *Hymn of the Universe*, Collins, London, 1965, p. 29.
[2] Cf. J. C., *Au colloque de l'Unesco Science et Synthèse*, LE MONDE, 17 December 1965, p. 13, col. 2.

a predilection for the glorious festivals of Christ, that of Christ the King (both cosmic Christ and evolutive Christ) and all the festivals revealing the divinity of Jesus—the Epiphany,[1] the Transfiguration, the Paschal resurrection and Ascension, which is the return of Christ to the bosom of the Father with the whole cosmos.

But let us leave the lofty spheres of mysticism. It is certain that, from some aspects, Teilhard was an exemplary priest, that he felt a missionary vocation and that the general temper of his thought is religious from beginning to end. It is true that Teilhard was often remote from what might be called normal ministry; how could he celebrate the Mass in the solitudes of the Gobi, or during the Yellow Expedition? But he was faithful to the recital of his breviary. Naturally, Teilhard never failed, year after year, to make his annual week's retreat, and his two notebooks of meditations afford overwhelming evidence of his fidelity to a specifically mystic vocation. Moreover, Teilhard celebrated the Mass with extraordinary fervour. As Madame Arsène-Henry testifies, "Anyone who never saw Teilhard celebrate Mass has seen nothing." Moreover, Father Teilhard in no way disdained to tell his beads, for this daring thinker retained a rare humility.

We repeat that Teilhard had a missionary soul. There again, certain appearances are deceptive. Teilhard, at first sight, never tried to convert, and with most of his geologist and palaeontologist colleagues, especially Chinese, he avoided talking religion. He was not a hunter of souls, and seems to have rigorously applied the *caritas discreta* of the Jesuits. The Chinese scientist, C. C. Young, was astonished to find this priest abstaining from all religious conversation, since Father Teilhard was not in the habit of acting systematically in the matter of faith. He liked to give free place to the action of the Holy Spirit, his attitude depending on the attitude and the preparation of the soul of the other person and the inner voice.

Teilhard deeply regretted not making conversions, but in fact he succeeded with a certain number, without being in any way a preacher. Conversions to Catholicism, of course; in spite of the discretion of the converts, a certain amount of evidence has finally reached me. The wife of a certain scientist, living in religious indifference, agreed to make her first communion. A certain Ambassador to the Far East, after reading LE MILIEU DIVIN, died reconciled to the faith. But Teilhard helped everyone to rise along their own lines. In China he

[1] Epiphany, in Greek, means manifestation.

got to know an American Jewess who had lost her faith; he advised her to re-read the Old Testament, and especially the Prophets.[1]

Furthermore, Teilhard, faithful to the Jesuit spirituality, possessed the love of youth—the interest which he took in young beginners is touching—and, above all, he conceived the formidable ambition of winning for Christ the modern world, the world of science and technology. This explains the boldness of his thought, his exceptional sensitiveness to the religious needs of his time, that astonishing attempt to speak only the language of the twentieth century and to project Christianity on the film of evolution. Teilhard, and this is one of the secrets of his influence, is one of the rare men who have really "tried" Christianity, lived and manifested in all its verity and explosive force. In his own fashion, Teilhard was a soul of the temper of St. Francis Xavier—whose tomb at Malacca he piously visited.

It is therefore not astonishing that Teilhard's thought is fundamentally theological in scope. Pastor Georges Crespy, in his Doctor's thesis on *La Pensée théologique de Teilhard de Chardin*[2] has given the final proofs of this. In fact we find in Teilhard the problematics of the theologian on certain points which he regards as vital, original sin, the Incarnation, the cosmic Christ, the Parousia, the Pleroma, and very specially the relation between Christic time (the time of revelation, properly so called) and historical time. But Teilhard's theology has this original feature, that it is embodied in a unitary design, in an overall view of the world, which is vision in cosmogenesis, whence the discomfiture of theologians accustomed to their own special technique.

And so, I come to the last theme of this line of thought: Teilhard is among the greatest apologists of the Christian religion. Naturally, the apologetics of the Dictionary of Apologetics never interested him, but he worked out an apologia of Christianity whose demonstrative power is comparable, and perhaps superior, to the thought of Pascal, Newman and Maurice Blondel. Can one imagine any more powerful argument in favour of Christianity than that of demonstrating how adaptable faith is to the modern vision in cosmogenesis, how capable that religion is, not only of becoming dynamic in contact with the modern world, but

---

[1] It should be added that the *Association des Amis de Pierre Teilhard de Chardin* is constantly recording authentic returns to Catholicism, returns which evidence the dimension of Teilhard's faith and authenticate his sanctity. The Gospel says "A tree shall be judged by its fruits."

[2] Paris and Brussels, Ed. Universitaires, 1961.

also of inspiring the universe of science and technology, and, finally, how apt Christianity is to become the universal religion by gathering back into itself the deviated or separated branches, the diverse Christianities, pantheisms and monisms, whose original sap and secular contributions it takes up and replaces in the vast orthodoxy of synthesis in which the equilibrium between extremes is to be realized in the final convergence?

. . . On the man of faith, we have merely suggested a mass of ideas which could be developed almost infinitely, since Teilhard, with his Christ the humanizer and the sanctifier, with his dynamic charity, represents the future of the Church, since he has reconciled it with the human. With regard to the scientist, we propose to follow an almost symmetrical line, apparently quite independent of the former. In the abstract, and as a first approximation, Teilhard's scientific career can be isolated and rapidly described.

His vocation as a geologist and naturalist was eminently pre-cocious. His father, Emmanuel, a gentleman farmer, horse lover, ornithologist and a great sportsman, loved nature. Very early he taught his son, Pierre, to observe the stars, to collect stones and minerals and to take an interest in insects and breed caterpillars. And this vocation steadily grew and developed. At the College of Mongré, Teilhard, although among the excellent pupils, was the despair of his master, Father Henri Bremond, because of his inattention in class. It was because he was dreaming of his beloved stones. When he reached the Philosophy Class, moreover, he went on short geological excursions in the Beaujolais with Father Desribes. After taking the Baccalaureat in Philosophy, he went on to take it in Elementary Mathematics. His novitiate and juvenate interrupted his scientific studies, but in Jersey he took advantage of all his free time to explore the island and study its tectonics. In Egypt he gave himself up to an ardent hunt for rare insects and fossils and made contact with researchers outside Egypt. In England, at Hastings, he explored the Weald, collected plants and fossil teeth and attracted the attention of various specialists.

So far, he had not gone beyond the amateur stage. But after his years of theology, he went to Paris to pursue his scientific studies. In 1912 he was introduced to Marcellin Boule, Professor of Palaeontology at the Museum of Natural History, joined his laboratory and made friends with the Abbé Breuil, already a great prehistorian, and began to take an interest in the origins of man. From then on the royal road

was open to the geologist and palaeontologist specializing in the Ceno-
zoic, and especially in the mammals.

To retrace this career would be to recount Teilhard's whole
biography, which was externally that of a research worker. I shall
content myself with a few comments: Teilhard was a man so gifted
that he started in research before even taking his "Licence" or first
degree, which he only took after the First World War. His departure
for China in 1923 was an unhoped chance, which opened with a brilliant
discovery, that of palaeolithic man in the Ordos.[1] By 1929 he was well
established as *persona grata* with the Chinese. In the 1930's, he is
already eminent as a scientist of international standing, and has
frequent contacts with the United States. He takes part in the excavations at Chou kou tien, near Peking, where the famous *Sinanthropus
pekinensis* was discovered. He was to stay in China until 1945, to join
the Institut in 1950, and, finally, to be "kidnapped" by the Americans
in 1951, who were to send him on two missions to South Africa in 1951
and 1953. On the whole, Teilhard's fame as a scientist, whatever
reservations may be entered on certain points of detail, is immense and
unchallenged, and lifts him on to the same plane[2] as men like Marcellin
Boule, Henri Breuil, V. K. Ting, Grabau, Barbour, Davidson Black or
Weidenreich. It is still impossible today to study the geology and palaeontology of China without attentively reading all his memoirs, which
constitute an irreplaceable contribution.

---

[1] In the great bend of the Yellow River. It is as well to recall that his
career as a European palaeontologist, though prematurely interrupted and
less spectacular, was equally important, if not more so.

[2] I am very careful to say "on the same plane" but in no way above them,
as the clumsy fanaticism of certain Teilhardians would tend to suggest.
It is true that in the letters to his cousin and in his TITRES ET TRAVAUX,
Teilhard did not sufficiently stress the role of his colleagues and his debt
towards them. Without Emile Licent in the first place and the Rockefeller
Foundation afterwards, he could have done nothing in China. But his
cousin Teillard-Chambon—whose culture was literary—was interested only
in him and not in his colleagues. As for his TITRES ET TRAVAUX, this is a
specifically French literary genre, in which the candidate is expected to
speak only of himself and not of others, a simple working convention and
not the sign of an absurd nationalism. In both cases Teilhard simply fell
in with what was expected of him, which in no way prevented him from
writing the obituaries of Davidson Black and Franz Weidenreich, in which
he refrained from speaking of himself, precisely because the convention is
the reverse.

Neither can there be any question of describing Teilhard's science or listing his scientific ideas.[1] It will be enough to call attention to a few points. Teilhard is not a positivist in the sense of the greybeards of the eighties and nineties, that is to say, he does not plaster the facts studied with an indigent philosophy which imagines that all that is knowable is derived from facts and experience, and that the rest is but battles of words, myth and poetry. But, while Teilhard is not a positivist, he certainly remains the most positive of scientists. "It is not a good thing", he wrote, "to have more ideas than facts", and he humorously and gently twitted the German–American scholar Grabau who, in the seclusion of his Peking villa, constructed ambitious theories on geological pulsations. He advised another scientist, Ralph von Koenigswald, to start by describing the facts with the greatest possible precision before giving his own interpretation in conclusion. There must be no confusion between personal views and statements of fact. Teilhard even carries caution to the extreme. In connexion with Chou kou tien, the great French prehistorian, Breuil, guaranteed the existence of bone tools which would be found in conjunction with the stone tools, and prepared a memoir on the subject.[2] But the presence of these bone tools might give rise to doubts and dis-

[1] What will surely survive of his are his ideas on man. Jean Rostand reproaches him with having made no contribution to the biochemical mechanisms of evolution. But palaeontology is not biochemistry, and constitutes an autonomous science, since fossils now meet up with calculus. It also has the great advantage not only of giving biochemistry a diachronic depth, but of bringing to light the major drives and the slow movements, as real as the others. It should further be recalled, as everyone knows, that Teilhard helped to renew palaeontology by giving it a more biological spirit—it was not for nothing that he worked in communion of ideas with the biologist Pierre Leroy, a pupil of Lucien Cuénot. Finally, it should be recalled, as is less well known, first, that Teilhard's study on the Siphneidae foreshadowed what was later achieved by Simpson, a synthesis between genetics and palaeontology, and, secondly, that in the closing years of his life, Teilhard wrote that if he had his time over again, he would specialize in biochemistry as the science capable of affording the keys to the mystery of life. In the great dispute between neo-Darwinism and neo-Lamarckism, the Jesuit scientist refused to take sides, thereby expressing the obscure uneasiness of French (Latin) scientists, who are beginning to sense that there are more things in heaven and earth than are dreamt of in the synthetic theory of evolution.

[2] It is, moreover, almost certain that Breuil, a first-class typologist, was right.

cussions, themselves capable of disturbing the Rockefeller Foundation which was subsidizing the excavations. Teilhard went so far as to oppose the publication of Breuil's memoir. "Never assert anything, unless you are sure" is the watchword of Teilhard's science. Teilhard is not a laboratory scientist, but an open-air scientist, who only breathes freely in the field.

Naturally, this positivity has never stopped Teilhard from finding ideas. All those who have observed him, and especially Barbour, have testified, first that he was a top-class observer, who saw things where others noticed nothing, an intuitive who could always disentangle the most involved geological intricacies, for example at Chou kou tien, who always discovered the axes on which the research effort should be concentrated and, finally, a man of general ideas, a synthetic spirit capable of brushing broad frescoes and opening up immense perspectives. The greatness and, to the non-specialist, the difficulty, of Teilhard, is precisely that a great many of his ideas are rooted in purely technical memoirs. When Teilhard asserts that evolution is irreversible, this is not a purely academic idea, but is buttressed by geological studies of the granitization of continents. In Teilhard's view, based on very precise analyses of Chinese geology, the continents are built progressively by the extension of the granite shelf which prevents their subsidence. Similarly with orthogenesis, the oriented addition of small mutations. Teilhard's views are supported, inter alia, by his celebrated and classical memoirs on the Siphneidae (rat-moles) of China, in which we find different species of *Siphneidae* following irreversible drives[1] as though there were a certain evolutive potential developing in the same direction. Similarly, the theory that evolution always tends towards greater consciousness, that it is an ascent of psychism, is not the pious affirmation of a noble believer in the spirit. This assertion is based on a mass of precise observations, from the evolution of the encephalon in horses, studied by Edinger, to the progressive evolution of the cranium observed in the different waves of mankind, so well described by Weidenreich. Teilhard has contributed to the development of what is called palaeo-neurology, that is to say, the study of the development of the encephalon through the animal world.

But that is not the most important thing. It is time to bring out two fundamental points. In the first place, Teilhard is thoroughly familiar with the language and mentality of the scientist, and secondly,

[1] The teeth do not grow continuously, the vertebrae merge, etc.

he has a passion for science, research and discovery. This first idea obviously amounts to a truism, but it is still striking to note the ease with which Teilhard moves in scientific circles the most impervious to Catholicism or Christianity. It is well known how cordial his relations were with the Chinese scientists, Ting, Pei, Young, whose agnosticism is complete, or with the freemason Rivet, the founder of the Musée de l'Homme, or with Sir Julian Huxley, the first Director-General of Unesco, the 'Pope of neo-Darwinism'. I say nothing of the touching affection displayed towards him by the fervent Presbyterian, Barbour. What is striking is the attachment to him of agnostics, whose liberty Teilhard profoundly respected, for he never tried *directly* to convert them, but awaited the opportunity to talk or to communicate his unpublished works. Young, who is now one of the established scientists of Communist China, has left some interesting recollections of Teilhard in which he expresses surprise that this Jesuit father never talked religion. As for Sir Julian Huxley, he has frequently borne witness to the extraordinary encounter between an atheist and a Jesuit on the plane of man and human convergence.[1]

Another point: what frequently struck Teilhard's companions was his passion for research. When he went into the field his face lit up, there was a special gleam in his eyes, he was animated with a sort of lightness of spirit, he came to life again. Why did Teilhard devote

[1] "Teilhard de Chardin was a notable pioneer in the great adventure of contemporary thought—modern man's attempt to integrate facts and ideas from every field of human knowledge and human activity to give a new and more comprehensive view of human destiny.

"In particular, Teilhard was one of the first to extend the concept of evolution so as to cover not only its biological phase but also its inorganic or cosmological and its cultural or psycho-social manifestations, thus attempting to bridge the gap between the material and the spiritual and to indicate guidelines for man's future direction.

"In this, though he did not, in my opinion, pay sufficient attention to the operative mechanisms underlying biological and cultural transformation, he has clearly indicated the type of bridge that needs to be built. Finally, he has stimulated the thought of professional theologians, philosophers and scientists, as well as of many thousands of young people, whether religiously or scientifically inclined, and set them searching for a larger and more firmly based truth."

(Hampstead, May 1965. Original text. German translation in PIERRE TEILHARD DE CHARDIN IN SELBSTZEUGNISSEN UND BILDDOKUMENTEN Dargestellt von Johannes Hemleben, Rowohlt, Reinbeck bei Hamburg, 1966, p. 165.)

himself to science? In obedience to an outdated spirituality, some Catholics take up science purely from good will, to render glory to God, to prove to the "Gentiles"[1] that the children of Heaven are as intelligent as the sons of Earth. There was nothing of all that in Teilhard. Some priests and religious devote themselves to science in order to obtain an adequate intellectual platform to tackle theological subjects, to reach a wider audience and acquire greater authority. This was true of Teilhard and he has clearly said so. But it is none the less true that Teilhard experienced an authentic vocation as a scientist going back to his childhood, and, if he sought, it was in order to *find*. Teilhard was a humble man, free from pride, but it is enough to skim his correspondence to find cries of triumph at every discovery. Teilhard can be said to have worn out his health in research, in which he showed an utter disdain for contingencies and drove his own body hard. From 1939 onwards his health was definitely affected.

One characteristic feature shows the extent to which Teilhard was a genuine scientist, namely his team spirit, his sense of collective work. First of all, from about 1929, he "went over" to the Chinese, recognizing that, with the Chinese nationalist drive, any scientific work would be impossible without the cooperation of the Chinese themselves, and, above all, he was very soon convinced that solitary work was becoming more and more impossible and vain. This was one of the reasons why he failed to get on with Father Licent, who had welcomed him at Tientsin and guided him in many expeditions in the Yellow River basin; Licent, an old campaigner, to whom Teilhard owed a great deal, was an individualist and treated the Chinese with a certain aloofness. Teilhard himself was constantly teamed up, with the Chinese, with the Scotsman Barbour, with the Americans, Andrews, de Terra, Movius, and he was never tempted to play the lone wolf. His conception of the ultra-human is thus based on specific experience. The ultra-human, for him, is the surpassing of humanity by virtue of co-reflexion, it is a society made unanimous, in which minds are reciprocally exalted and enriched, where there reigns a sort of conspiracy of hearts. Now, it is by virtue of his scientific experience that Teilhard understood how greatly a well directed socialization can bring about the rebound of human evolution.

*　　　*　　　*

[1] The unbelievers.

The keynote of the first part of this survey has been dissociation, the mystic on the one side, the scientist on the other. We have followed the rules of analysis. But Teilhard was above all a man of synthesis. Madeleine Barthélemy-Madaule has made the point well. "In fact the controlling idea in Teilhard consists in a reflection upon his scientific thought (experiment and hypothesis); a reflection on his religious experience (personal experience and the situation of religion); a synthetic reflection governing and uniting the first two. It is in the latter that the philosophical moment, the dialectical process, is found."[1] Therefore we shall now regroup the elements we have distinguished and rank them in a single organic unity.

In face of the delicate problem of the relations between science and faith, there is a twofold temptation which must be overcome. The first would evade a solution, the second would result in a hasty, facile solution. One would lead to schizophrenia, the other to literalism and the Action Fatima.[2] I will explain myself.

First, watertight compartments, the laboratory on one side, the oratory on the other. There is nothing to distinguish the Christian scientist from his agnostic colleagues. In the laboratory his behaviour is exactly the same and his technical memoirs are indistinguishable from those of other men. Everything is governed by obedience to facts, to experience, and by the critical sense, for everything is constantly challenged. In contrast, in the oratory, *homo sapiens* becomes *homo religiosus*, and humbly and passively accepts the teaching of the Church, to which he submits without any critical examination. In short, a positivist plus a fideist, two equally untenable positions.[3] In the humorous words of Canon Raven:[4] "The theologians still discourse as if the music of the spheres or even of the fiddles had no necessary relationship with the instruments that transmit it, while the scientists in their professional capacity still insist (. . .) that the only explanation of a violin concerto must be in terms of 'the scraping of the tails of horses on the intestines of cats'."

[1] RÉFLEXIONS SUR LA MÉTHODE ET LA PERSPECTIVE TEILHARDIENNES.
[2] A French integrist movement, hostile to Teilhard.
[3] Cf. Pierre Smulders, LA VISION DE TEILHARD DE CHARDIN, 2nd ed. Paris, Desclée de Brouwer, 1965, p. 33: "The believing scientist suffers from a sort of intellectual schizophrenia, which in turn becomes a menace to faith." This was true in the case of Pasteur.
[4] TEILHARD DE CHARDIN, SCIENTIST AND SEER, London, Collins, 1962, p. 22.

Our picture is, of course, a caricature, but this tendency towards *homo duplex* certainly exists. Some French scientists frequent the Catholic Centre of French Intellectuals but take care not to compromise themselves with philosophy and theology. Sometimes this compartmentation takes more subtle forms. I am thinking now of the remarkable little book by Georges Gusdorf, SCIENCE ET FOI AU MILIEU DU XXe SIÈCLE. The author very rightly asserts the autonomy of science and of faith each in their own proper sphere. There are two readings of the world, one of science and the other of faith. These two readings in no way interfere with each other. Everyone knows the saying of Ambroise Paré[1] "The treatment was mine, but the healing was God's". The practitioners do everything needed to care for the sick and the physiological determinisms come into play. That is the first reading. But this healing, when it is unexpected, unhoped for, may, in the eyes of the faithful, be transformed into a sign and interpreted as divine intervention. That is the second reading. And the two readings do not interfere with each other. No-one challenges the validity of the scientific explanation, but it remains a foreground, a façade, behind which it is the hand of God which acts. In the cosmic drama the leading actor remains invisible, and his initiatives are always unexpected and gratuitous. It is rather like *Athaliah*.[2] The High Priest Joad is a subtle politician who understands how to bring psychological forces into play and entice Athaliah into a cunningly devised snare, a trap to make a policeman or a revolutionary green with envy. And yet, the leading actor, whose invisible hands govern all, is God.

Another solution is concordism. This time, there is really an attempt at a solution. For the concordist, there is no possible conflict between science and faith, faith being predominant. For the concordist, the cosmological assertions of the Bible can be made to correspond almost term for term with the theories of science. For example, GENESIS shows us God creating the world in six days. Very well, these six days fairly accurately symbolize the great periods of world history. Non-living matter began by organizing itself, land and water were separated, and plants, animals and man appeared in succession, science in no way forbidding belief in an original couple.

Of course the time is past when Father Mersenne, the good religious and friend of Descartes and admirer of Galileo, could calculate the

[1] A famous French surgeon of the XVIe century.
[2] Jean Racine's play.

tonnage of Noah's Ark. According to the good Father, the Bible was right. The proof is that the Ark was big enough to hold all the animals of Creation with ease. But this caricature of concordism is not entirely dead. As Action-Fatima-France says with all seriousness in its pamphlet printed in opposition to Teilhard,[1] after a review of modern palaeontology: "After these findings we have re-read the three first Chapters of Genesis and we have seen that the history of the earth and of creation followed by the Fall, as we have succeeded in reconstituting it by the scientific method, corresponds to the facts revealed to us by the Bible story of creation and the consequences of the fault of the first human couple. We have concluded from this that creation was a fact and that the stories of Creation and Fall in Genesis set out the history of the origins of earth, life and man."—The concordist, even if his style is less desperately flat than that of the Fatimite sect, therefore nurses a particular concept of the Bible, which he regards as having been revealed *en bloc*, dictated, as it were, by the Holy Spirit, and imagines that revelation, constituting a closed circle, stops short with the Bible.

But the concordist solution presents grave difficulties, even if one confines oneself to the relatively acceptable forms of concordism, such as regarding Canon Lemaître's celebrated theory of the expanding universe as scientific confirmation of the theological concept of creation.[2] It very soon becomes apparent, even to the unenlightened, that the parallel between the Bible and science is artificial and even false.[3] The creation of the world *in six days* is probably a liturgical recital intended to justify the institution of the Sabbath. There is nothing scientific about it. As for the famous story of Joshua stopping the sun, if you take it literally,[4] it purely and simply contradicts the elementary truths as taught by elementary school teachers the world over. To try

---

[1] 1962, p. 78.

[2] There is, of course, another cosmological theory, the steady state theory, which assumes a universe unlimited in space and time and in statistical equilibrium. It is true that Lemaître's hypothesis has been brilliantly taken up by Gamow and that the balance seems to lean in its favour. But the theological concept of creation, namely a certain relation of dependence of the participated being on God, has nothing to do with an astronomical theory and does not depend upon it.

[3] On this problem, cf. Haag, Haas, Hürzeler, EVOLUTION UND BIBEL, Luzern und München, Rex-Verlag, 3rd edition, 1963.

[4] As the adherents of Action-Fatima still venture to do.

to justify Biblical cosmology is to confound inspiration with dictation. The Holy Spirit never *dictated* the sacred books, it *inspired* them, that is to say, impelled the authors to make a certain number of assertions of a metaphysical and theological nature about God, man's destiny and the relations between God and mankind. But the Holy Spirit has fully respected the mentality of the Jews, with their pre-scientific cosmology, their literary *genres* and their virtual incapacity to express abstract ideas, to such an extent that the Bible can be the subject of a human science, an exhaustive philological criticism, which in no way changes the metaphysical assertions, which do not fall within the realm of philology, whose only object is to establish the text and avoid misconstructions. On a certain plane the Bible can be analysed by the same methods as the Veda or the Koran.

Having regard to the pre-scientific character of the Bible it is somewhat amusing to note that "Marxist astrophysicists reject the hypothesis of an expanding universe, as they reject the general extension of the principle of dissipation of energy (. . .), precisely because the hypothesis of an expanding universe implies (. . .) a time t_o, a beginning of time, an age of the Universe. The Universe would have commenced some billions of years ago. The extension and generalization of the principle of dissipation of energy to the whole Universe foreshadows a thermal death of the Universe. (. . .) These hypotheses, which lead the mind to the idea of a beginning and end of the Universe, seem to the Marxist scientists and philosophers to incline the mind dangerously towards the Jewish and Christian idea of creation. According to Marxist cosmology and ontology, in effect, the world is eternal, infinite in space and time, because uncreated."[1] Marxists are still nourished on an outdated and a degenerate catechism.

Once a distinction is drawn between dictation and inspiration,[2] a whole mass of false problems vanish in smoke, and we see the full error of the Inquisition in condemning Galileo. This was, moreover, the thinking of Teilhard, who considered that many of the figurative stories in the Bible are merely an effort to express metaphysical truths, to render the ineffable. Teilhard, the man of synthesis, could not resign himself to compartmentation, even though he accepted the

[1] Claude Tresmontant, LETTRE (Paris), September–October 1962, p. 20.
[2] This inspiration does not exclude a certain infallibility, since in each age God has given men to understand the maximum they are able to comprehend.

D

idea of the necessary autonomy of the two orders of knowledge. But, as is proved by a letter which I cite in the conclusion to my large work,[1] Teilhard as a man of science could not tolerate the naiveties of concordism either, even though it clumsily expressed a truth, namely that an ultimate antagonism between science and faith remains impossible.[2] What, then, is Teilhard's solution?

Teilhard's answer is extremely complex and extremely rich. Let us try to define all its aspects.

It is enough to refer to COMMENT JE CROIS (1934) and to the extra-ordinary biography constituted by LE COEUR DE LA MATIÈRE (1950) to describe the experience to which Teilhard surrendered himself with all the sincerity, loyalty and fervour of his soul. He was at the same time a child of Earth and a son of Heaven. He loved the rugged earth, the γῆ μήτηρ, *the Terra Mater* with a love as total and as pure as his love of Christ, and he allowed the two halves of his soul to react freely on one another until he had obtained inner unity, that intoxicating vision in which God-Ahead, the God of evolution, the *Deus evolutivus* and God-Above, the transcendent God of GENESIS, are revealed as one, as the two faces of the same God, the unity being achieved through Christ, more precisely through the cosmic Christ, the evolutive Christ.

---

[1] TEILHARD DE CHARDIN by Claude Cuénot, London, Burns and Oates, 1965, p. 395. Cf. the important letter of 14 April 1953: "Avoid like the plague any kind of 'concordism' which would try to bring together and to justify by each other what is possibly only a momentary representation of dogma with what is possibly also only a momentary phase of scientific vision." Cf. also, COMMENT JE VOIS, 1948, p. 1: "We must be careful not to confound '*concordism*' with '*coherence*', " and the letter of 30 April 1948: "The error of Concordism is to confound the meridians in the region of the Equator (the meridian of Science and the meridian of Faith). But these meridians must unite somewhere at a Pole (if one looks, scientifically and religiously, at the Whole)—that is to say, they must obey certain general conditions of structuration (such as the organic laws of union); and it is only this *coherence* (not concordance) that I defend." (Cited by E. Rideau, LA PENSÉE DU PÈRE TEILHARD DE CHARDIN, Paris, Editions du Seuil, 2nd edition, 1965, pp. 25–26, n. 1.)

[2] Pierre Smulders (LA VISION DE TEILHARD DE CHARDIN, Paris, Desclée, 2nd ed., 1965, pp. 58–59) has opportunely recalled that at all times there have been anti-concordist reactions. For example, St. Athanasius recall-ed that light (the first day) could not have been created before the sun and the moon (fourth day).

We read in the Foreword to COMMENT JE CROIS:[1] "The originality of my belief is that it is rooted in two spheres of life which are generally regarded as antagonistic. By upbringing and intellectual training I belong to 'the children of Heaven'. But by temperament and by professional studies I am a 'child of Earth'. Thus, placed by life in the heart of two worlds whose theory, language and sentiment I know from familiar experience, I have raised no inner barrier. But I have allowed two apparently contrary influences to react on each other in full freedom in the depths of my being. Now, at the term of this operation, after thirty years devoted to the pursuit of inner unity, I have the impression that a synthesis has come about naturally between the two streams which beckoned me. The one has not destroyed, but reinforced the other." And in the third part of LE COEUR DE LA MATIÈRE, Teilhard reverts to this theme: "The cosmic sense and the Christic sense: in me, two axes apparently independent of each other in their birth, and whose connexion of convergence and ultimate identity of substance I have ended by grasping, only after much time and effort, through and beyond the Human."

This synthesis was not to come about without pain and inner conflict. During his novitiate he was on the brink of renouncing the study of stones to devote himself entirely to directly religious activities. It was the robust common sense of the Master of the Novices, Father Troussard, which rescued him from this crisis by obliging him to hold both ends of the chain. Later, in Egypt, Teilhard experienced the converse temptation of becoming lost in nature and dissolving himself in the elemental. But these youthful crises were overcome quickly enough, and in virtually permanent fashion. Faith in the world, faith in God, faith in Christ, were to remain closely associated. That is precisely what makes Teilhard's experience an exemplary model. Teilhard, in effect, gained by his experience; a Jesuit priest and a profound mystic, he lived almost always in a scientific environment and in a fundamentally non-Christian universe. He might, as it were, have remained bilingual and contented himself with the complete mastery of both languages with equal ease. It is true that, when he likes, he makes use sometimes of one and sometimes of the other

[1] There are innumerable passages in Teilhard on the problem of science and faith, from SCIENCE ET CHRIST (1921) to RECHERCHE, TRAVAIL ET ADORATION (1955, cf. Section 2: *Le conflit religion-science et sa solution*) including *Le Christianisme et la Science*, ESPRIT, 1946.

idiom, without confusion. But in fact, in many cases, he has contrived
to speak one language in such a way that the others can understand,
and vice versa.

In a letter of the 19 June 1926,[1] he wrote to his cousin: "The day
before yesterday, before a mixed audience of Chinese and Americans,
a very likeable Harvard professor gave a simple and modest explanation of how he understood the dawn of thought in the animal series.
I couldn't help thinking of the abyss that divides the intellectual world
I was in and whose language I knew, from the theological world of
Rome with whose idiom I am also familiar. At first it was something of
a shock to realize that the latter could be, and indeed must be, just as
real as the former; and then I told myself that now perhaps I was
capable of so using the first language as to make it fairly express what
the other contains but puts into words that most people can no longer
understand."

This is exactly what Teilhard tried to do. Except in his purely
technical memoirs, Teilhard's concepts, when he is speaking as a
scientist, have metaphysical overtones. Conversely, when the mystic
speaks, his vocabulary is full of scientific terms and metaphors.

As Jean Onimus has well observed:[2] "An immense effort to trans-
late into a common language what he felt to be the two faces of the
same reality. It must be said that it was from a passionate love of his
faith that Teilhard transgressed the sphere of scientific research and
dared to be philosopher and theologian at once. If he had remained
content to be a scientist he could have lived in Paris crowned with
honours and ended up in the Collège de France." In this, Teilhard
followed the advice of the Superior of "Etudes", the "divine Léonce",
alias Father Léonce de Grandmaison: "It would be an immense service,
and a very well spent life's work, to integrate the results, suggestions
and interpretations which guide modern scientists into Christian philosophy, or even into negatively Christian philosophy, that is to say
philosophy consistent with the Christian life."

Let us try to look a little more closely.

It is quite evident that Teilhard's faith is adapted to his science
—facile, and, if one may say so, spectacular developments. But to

[1] LETTRES DE VOYAGE, Paris, Grasset, ed. 1956 pp. 91–92. English translation, LETTERS FROM A TRAVELLER, Collins, 1962, p. 127.
[2] PIERRE TEILHARD DE CHARDIN OU LA FOI AU MONDE, Paris, Plon 1963,
p. 19.

shrink from facility is a misplaced modesty. This direct or indirect action of science on faith has a great many aspects which we shall try to list.

Everyone knows the two problems on which science and faith are always clashing, namely miracles and original sin, or more accurately, *peccatum originans*, that is to say, original sin considered at its source, at the dawn of historic humanity. Let us start with miracles. In the old days they were one of the mainsprings of apologetics.

"And what age was ever so fruitful in miracles?" asks Joad in *Athaliah*.[1] But it certainly seems that with modern man, even with Catholics, the miracle has lost much of its apologetic value and is hardly convincing any longer. A Catholic philosopher,[2] perfectly pious and sincere, even went so far as to say that he believed, not because of, but in spite of, miracles, which reflects the secret thought of many believers.[3] There is certainly a very powerful apologetics in Teilhard, recently studied by Father Christian d'Armagnac S.J.,[4] but miracles play no part in it. In the work LA FOI QUI OPÈRE (1918)[5] Teilhard tells us that Jesus came to bring us "not only a new life, superior to that of

[1] L. 104.

[2] Edouard Le Roy.

[3] Cf. Teilhard—LE CHRISTIANISME DANS LE MONDE (1933) Section 5 (*La Religion de demain*): "Without denying, but quite the contrary, the possibility, or even the likelihood in the neighbourhood of the *true* Religion, of an unexpected relaxation of determinisms, due to some super-animation of Nature under the influence of a divine radiation, we must clearly recognize that the consideration of miracles has ceased to act effectively on our minds. Their acceptance raises so many historical or physical difficulties that there are probably many Christians who at present remain believers not *because*, but *in spite* of the prodigies related in the Scriptures."

[4] *La Pensée du Père Teilhard de Chardin comme Apologétique moderne*, NOUVELLE REVUE THÉOLOGIQUE, Louvain, June 1962, pp. 598–621. The work of Maurice Corvez O.P., DE LA SCIENCE À LA FOI TEILHARD DE CHARDIN, Tours, Mame, 1964, 190 pp., is an apologetics partly inspired by Teilhard and makes no great new contribution. See also Henri de Lubac, *Note sur l'apologétique teilhardienne*, in LA PRIÈRE DU PÈRE TEILHARD DE CHARDIN, Paris, Fayard, 1964, pp. 149–222; PIERRE TEILHARD DE CHARDIN, TÉMOIN DE LA FOI, Paris, Bloud et Gay–Desclée de Brouwer, 1968. Coll. TÉMOINS' DE LA FOI. Cf. also, H. de Lubac, S.J., TEILHARD MISSIONNAIRE ET APOLOGISTE, Toulouse, Ed. Prière et Vie, 1966 (pp. 55–110).

[5] ÉCRITS DU TEMPS DE LA GUERRE (1916–1919), Paris, Grasset, 1965, pp. 319, 320 and 323.

which we are conscious—but also a very real new physical power of acting on our temporal World. (. . .) Fundamentally, the Christian has received from his Saviour the power to conquer Fortune, that is to say, to make the chances favourable to himself. (. . .) No doubt, there is a *Faith in miracles*. But it should not mislead us as to the true nature of our spiritual empire over the cosmos.—The *prodigy*—which astonishes us because it forces determinisms in a limited space, and *'locally'* reverses the march of Time—has always been and certainly seems destined to remain, an exceptional means of action. The anticipation or the reflexion of a form of life transcending our own, it does not seem, in any way, to be the dawn of a terrestrial state of liberation and well-being.[1] (. . .) Normally, in its habitual action (. . .)—which is all that concerns us here—Faith does not break the evil links irrevocably contracted in the past. It merely *integrates* them in a higher order. It forces them to serve the good. It transforms them, it *absorbs* them. The believer, *if he has faith*, can bring sickness and the fault in which the pusillanimous founder, into a combination from which *his* Universe issues more sanctifying and more divine."

Operative faith therefore appears as a victory over hazard: "Finally, *the disorder, the changes*, among which we move, are revealed as a pure appearance. The chaotic figure of the Future is due to the fact that we see the Universe forming 'backwards' or 'upside down'. It is a tapestry looked at from the back, or a piece of music played in reverse. The movement of events, if it is to appear harmonious, must be looked at in due order, that is to say starting from the results which they have been animated to produce."[2] Looked at in this way (that is to say, starting from God, who brings us back to him) not only do their troops become ordered, but they appear cemented in a Finality (proportionate to our Faith) which gives their apparent mobility a coherence greater than that of the Past. Contrary to our habitual impression, *everything here below holds together from above*. Thus, therefore, the miracle (in the sense of the prodigy in the physical world) is merely a very special case of 'operative faith' and, except for that

[1] Furthermore, Teilhard did not regard prodigies (apart from the miracles of Christ) as a negation of the laws of nature, but as a sort of activation, of super-animation, in which natural processes are not negated but accelerated, which is not at all the same thing. See above, the quotation from CHRISTIANISME DANS LE MONDE.

[2] Sic, *ibidem*, p. 322.

sort of anticipation of the Pleroma constituted by the miracles of Christ,[1] it merely represents a super-animation of natural phenomena (a sort of catalysis due to the action of the supernatural). In any event a miracle is only meaningful to the eyes of faith.

Another point of direct friction is the origins of man. Here again, Teilhard must not be imagined as a revolutionary "putting a red bonnet on the head of the old Denziger". In the first place, he tells us, biological science is never concerned with individuals, it only recognizes populations. In consequence, in the strict sense, palaeontology has no authority to deny outright the existence of an original couple. There is also a law, defined by Teilhard, of the disappearance of peduncles: the origins of all things are generally unspectacular and very discreet and they disappear. Who can boast today of having at home the ancestor of the bicycle? This is particularly true for the origin of species. Generally, at the start, individuals are relatively few in number, very atypical and not highly specialized. The rhinoceros horn started as a simple boss, the trunk of the *Proboscidea* was originally very short. It is a marvel that we have discovered the *Archaeopteryx*, the inter-mediary between the reptiles and the birds, and it represented an already highly developed type of bird. It is not exactly the "missing link". It is an even greater marvel that Jean Piveteau should have discovered the *Protobatrachus*, thereby clearing up the riddle of the origin of the *Anura*. Thus, therefore, at the origin of species, we find a blank. This may, at a pinch,[2] leave room for the speculations of theologians. Finally, Teilhard in no way ruled out the historical exist-ence of individual faults. He asserted that all men have been, are and will be, tainted by sin. His position therefore is that the scientists on one side and the theologians on the other, must each take a step

----

[1] It is also as well to recall that Jesus would not descend from the Cross and refused, both to the Tempter and to the Jews, to effect prodigies on a cosmic scale (to leap from the top of the Temple or change the course of the stars).

[2] We say "at a pinch". In fact, as Roger Garaudy points out: "One of the great classical temptations of Christian apologetics is to insert God and the supernatural, both good and evil, in the temporary gaps in human knowledge. Under this method, theology is always the loser, in proportion as our knowledge grows. Teilhard deliberately declined to make God, in the words of Father Dubarle: 'the small substitution for our intellectual insufficiencies'." (Cf. *Un entretien de Tanneguy de Quénétain avec R.G.* RÉALITÉS (Paris), May 1966, p. 100, col. 1.)

forward to meet each other, which implies reciprocal understanding.

This being said, Teilhard, like all scientists, Catholic or not, regarded monogenism as scientifically improbable. An original couple, however restricted the zone of hominizing mutation might appear at the outset, seemed to him highly unlikely. How could such a singular mutation have had a chance of survival? The use of long bones as clubs, of the antlers of deer as daggers, the manipulation of barely flaked stones was not enough to guarantee survival in the face of all the chances of destruction. Furthermore, grave sin, the rejection of the prevenient grace of God, presuppose an enormous progress in human reflection, a mental level which the first hominids had certainly not reached. As was said by Abbé Henri Breuil, a priest of the utmost fidelity and devotion to his faith—it was he who stopped Cardinal Merry del Val from fulminating forth a wholesale condemnation of evolutionism—man started as a baby, an infantile creature. How could *Sinanthropus*, who was already a highly developed man, have conceived the idea of deicide? Even at the level of the Neanderthaloids, who already followed religious practices and buried their dead in grottoes to neutralize their powers, even at this level such a concept remains unthinkable.[1]

Teilhard did not profess to have the alternative solution or the final answer. He never laid down the law or pontificated. He simply suggested lines of research. He seems to have rejected the historical existence of an original couple. He also rejects the more or less Neo-Platonic solution of a pre-cosmic Adam, of a fall anterior to the appearance of historic humanity, the burden of which falls upon them. He thought this unverifiable solution too metaphysical, and seeming to suggest that the appearance of the cosmos issued from a sort of catastrophe of the absolute. *Peccatum originans*, in the eyes of Teilhard, is cosmic and collective, the sin of the world. In a certain fashion, evil is linked structurally, not with the many, which is neither good nor evil, but with a world in evolution, in cosmogenesis, in the course of unification, since failure is always possible and a world in genesis is always fragile. To this is added, on the conscious plane, the temptation called

---

[1] A good Roman Catholic theologian, Fr. A. Vaneste, has written, 'the classical presentation of the dogma has the appearance of a childish fable which the modern world can no longer take seriously', cited in R. Rouquette, *Un discours du Pape sur le péché originel*, ÉTUDES, October 1966, p. 385.

Promethean[1] since sin appears with the liberty of man. Man, being the first living being with a psychism fully integrated in a personal synthesis and forming, as Teilhard says, the first being with a "punctiform"[2] (and not diffused) psychism could not help suffering the temptation (fatal for him) of believing himself to be completed and perfect, of erecting himself into an entirely closed system and rejecting the idea that everything is a gift of God. In short, through the whole structure of cosmogenesis, there was a great temptation for man to divinize himself. Sin, that is to say conscious and deliberately willed evil, the rejection of the love of God, therefore results from a cosmic structure, since it is evolutive.

Man, summoned to the beatific union, is a wayfarer. He possesses neither his God nor his happiness fully in himself. He is therefore fallible, tempted by everything which gives him the illusion of this beatitude. He desires immediately what he can only obtain tomorrow. Man desires his happiness in advance of and in a different manner from, God's design. The fact nevertheless remains that modern science finds it hard to admit the exceptional gravity of the sin committed by the first humans and capable of unleashing a universal catastrophe, since sin, like responsibility, has various degrees, full responsibility requiring full consciousness.[3]

Furthermore, sin has a collective aspect. Man is bound up not only with the universe, but with man. Naturally, individual faults remain individual, but not to mention their social repercussions, always more or less great, they wound not only the individual, they wound man, the human, as a concrete universal. They wound mankind, which is one, and clearly constitutes the single Adam to whom St. Paul alludes.[4]

[1] We take Prometheanism in the pejorative sense, the sense which inspired the Tower of Babel, the first manifestation in collectivized man of the tendency to deicide. But it is as well to recall that the Prometheus of Aeschylus is the most religious of men and adores the "God-Ahead", the God of progress. His love of mankind contrasts singularly with the obscurantist and reactionary God, Zeus.

[2] That is to say, integrated and unified.

[3] The *Epistle to the Hebrews* (X. 26–31) speaks of sin *after Christ* as essentially more serious.

[4] Cf. G. Crespy, DE LA SCIENCE À LA THÉOLOGIE, ESSAI SUR TEILHARD DE CHARDIN, Neuchâtel, Ed. Delachaux et Niestlé, 1965, p. 82: "What is Biblical (. . .) is the idea of the *solidarity* of the group, what Wheeler Robinson has called the idea of 'corporate personality'. According to this

The Germans, in their concentration camps, experimented with the cooling and warming of the human body, experiments which were in fact concealed torture. In the film *Victor and Vanquished* we find them carrying out these sadistic manipulations even on children. Now, when we look at one of these unfortunate victims, with their frozen feet, their lifeless legs, we feel a stab in our own heart. It is because this dehumanization of the executioner dehumanizes all mankind, that is to say, each one of us. In a certain sense we are all involved in the death camps, Nazi or Stalinist.

Thus, therefore, original sin, for Teilhard, while preserving its personal dimension, becomes cosmic[1] and collective. Henceforth, it is no longer possible to dissociate ourselves from the first sinful men, to protest against this "hereditary" sin for which we considered ourselves individually irresponsible. We can no longer wash our hands of them, not only because each of us, on his own account, revives original sin, but because sin is cosmic and collective and one cannot dissociate oneself from the cosmos and humanity, even when one is a schizophrenic. It follows that baptism, far from losing its importance, becomes even more urgent. Teilhard is certainly one of those who have reopened the problem of original sin, who have made it possible to distinguish between the truth enshrined in dogma and its trappings, and who have suggested lines of research. It is for the theologians to prolong and clarify this trial with their own techniques—which they have, moreover, already started to do. Is there any exegetist who is unaware that, in the Bible, *Adam* is, in 85% of cases, a plural, a collective noun?[2]

Miracles and original sin constitute, in the eyes of the common

idea, the individual represents the whole group, in space and in time, and, reciprocally, the entire group is responsible for the individual. In other words, no human act, good or bad, is the isolated act of an *individual* alone, every act involves the group and, in extreme cases, because of the interconnections between groups, all mankind."

[1] No-one has challenged the cosmic character of Redemption. The sin of man is therefore truly cosmic in its whole essence (and not merely through its consequences).

[2] Cf. G. Crespy, *op. cit.* p. 82: "The hypothesis that a first couple is responsible for the sins of mankind because of the inheritance of acquired characteristics by a single act, is wholly unacceptable, at any rate in that form. It is, moreover, not Biblical, for *Adam*, in the Old Testament, as in the New, is not the name of an individual, but a generic term, and the idea of the inheritance of faults, by way of biological descent, is likewise not a Biblical idea."

or average believer or unbeliever, zones of direct friction and sources of uneasiness on questions of fact. Teilhard has raised the debate on to a higher plane. The conflict can only arise in two cases, where a misguided science meddles in laying down the law on questions of a metaphysical character, or where a misguided theology confounds the truth enshrined in dogma with its trappings, more or less representational and provisional—it being clearly borne in mind that it is quite possible for science and theology to be simultaneously misguided. As Newman has noted:[1] "(. . .) if anything seems to be proved by astronomer, or geologist, or chronologist, or antiquarian, or ethnologist, in contradiction to the dogmas of faith, that point will eventually turn out, first, *not* to be proved, or secondly, not *contradictory*, or thirdly, not contradictory to anything *really revealed*, but to something which has been confused with revelation."

But these two special cases in fact remain very secondary, arising, as they do, from a misunderstanding.[2] The great merit of Teilhard is to have demonstrated that the scientific spirit (and no longer only on questions of fact) may have the most profound repercussions on the language of faith, without, however, thereby modifying its essence. I mean by the scientific spirit a certain set of mental attitudes and cosmological representations which I shall try to clarify, analyse and classify methodically.

The scientific spirit is, first of all, demythification, the rejection of myth, of everything which is fabulation or confabulation, figure of speech or uncriticised metaphor. Teilhard's religion is a religion largely stripped of psychological archaisms, which endeavours to distinguish between the object of faith and the cosmological representations, the outdated stories, through which the faith has been transmitted to us. Teilhard is well aware, for example, that the Bible—Old and New Testament—is the revelation of the mystery of God in a *human* language. He has therefore adopted that concept which is fundamental to exegesis, that of mentality, namely that revelation is always expressed through a given cultural complex and never in a pure state. ✓

[1] THE IDEA OF A UNIVERSITY DEFINED AND ILLUSTRATED, London, Longmans, Green and Co., 5th ed. 1885. Part 2. University subjects: VIII. Christianity and Scientific Investigation.
[2] As has been well said by Roger Garaudy: "Teilhard (. . .) has tried to eject theology from the domain of science." (Cf. *Un entretien de Tanneguy de Quénétain* avec R.G. RÉALITÉS (Paris), May 1966, p. 100, col. 1.)

God speaks through men whose personality, and therefore whose thought and language, he respects. Revelation is the seed sown in mankind which, in accordance with the law of evolution, it must progressively develop. Some husks of the seed must fall, neither too early nor too late. Science, all science, is the condition of the sound development of theology.[1]

Teilhard, as we have seen, is a mystic, and a non-figurative mystic. Now, a typical example of the non-mythical character of Teilhard's religion is his devotion to the Sacred Heart. The essence of mysticism is union with God, profound and as total and perpetual as possible. It is born of the accord between the will of God and the will of man, the latter, in a complete surrender *of love*, allowing the spiritual organism received at baptism, that is to say, the theological virtues of faith, hope and charity, and the gifts of the Holy Spirit, to operate in it more and more fully. In fact, Teilhard's life was a perpetual communion with God, not only through the Eucharist, but through people and beings. It was God whom he never ceased to savour, it was for the risen Christ (who, by eucharistization progressively assimilates the earth and the universe to himself) that Teilhard constantly tightened his links with his familiars, his workmates and his travelling companions, realizing the goal of all love, uninterrupted unity, the prelude to eternal life. This unity being the fruit of love, Teilhard discovered and passionately loved its source, the very Heart of the Word incarnate, from which gushes the Spirit of fire, the Spirit of consummation, of the unity of love, the Third Person of the Trinity. The Heart of Christ expresses the mystery of the love of God in itself and in the universe. It is the focus of universal Energy, the cause and the purpose of the world, the source of all energy. Teilhard is therefore well in the line of this mysticism of the consummation of love.[2] We have come a long way from the popular imagery of the flaming Heart crowned with thorns.

[1] Cf. Pius XII, address of 25 April 1955, to the members of the Pontifical Academy of Sciences: "While it is the duty of science to seek its own self-consistency and to draw its inspiration from sound philosophy, such philosophy must never profess to determine the truths which are derived solely from experience and the scientific method. In effect, only experience, understood in the widest sense, can indicate which among the infinite variety of possible magnitudes and material laws are those which the Creator has willed to realize." (cf. OSSERVATORE ROMANO, 25–26 April 1955.)
[2] The door of which has been open since the beginnings, from the *Song of Songs* to St. Bernard and St. John of the Cross.

Teilhard has demythified because he has plumbed the depths of what was perceived only on the surface, because in making the fontal light blaze forth, he has eliminated superstition and deviation. He has made religion adult, he has fulfilled it instead of diminishing it, and it is for that reason that he is at the antipodes of the modernism which has gradually gnawed away the Scriptures without safeguarding or augmenting the living seed which they contain.

Next, the scientific spirit is the spirit of research. The scientist worthy of the name (I am not talking of some of the established pontiffs) has a mind which is in a state of constant revolt. His master virtue is uneasiness. *Mutatis mutandis*, Baudelaire's lines can be applied to him:

"Forced by the restless flame that burns our brain,
Needs must we plumb the depths or scale the heights,
Indifferent to Heaven or Hell, so be we reach
The heart of the unknown and find—the New!"

It is true that scientists have always displayed serious weaknesses. At certain moments they have imagined that their science was complete. This was the case, for example, with the pre-Einstein and pre-quantum-physics of the end of the nineteenth century, before the discovery of radium by the Curies. The pontiffs, when they have their hands on the controls, seek to impose an orthodoxy and will not tolerate heretical disciples, those who shake their theories and display an awkward originality. But these stabilities, these orthodoxies are always set in motion again and collapse under the pressure of research. A theory which has been shaken by the facts does not survive its author, or is integrated with vaster perspectives. Now, for Teilhard, who lived in a state of tension, a tension wholly powerful and prudent at the same time, sustained by faith, there is an *absolute* duty of research. As early as 1916, in LA MAÎTRISE DU MONDE ET LE RÈGNE DE DIEU, he wrote: "(. . .) *not to search*, not to plumb to the depth the domain of Energies and Thought, not to try to fathom the Real, would be *a grave threefold fault*: a *fault of infidelity* towards the Master who has placed Man in the heart of Things to see him consciously and freely prolong their immanent Evolution and his creative work; a *fault of presumption* which would make them *tempt God*, hoping to gain by indolent prayer, Revelation or Miracle, what could be won by natural work; finally, also, *a lack of intellectual integrity. . . ."*[1] And the month before his death, in March 1955, Teilhard wrote a paper under the title *Recherche, travail et adoration.*

The concept of religious research is derived immediately from this absolute duty of research. It is, of course, not an entirely new concept. Exegesis does not cease to progress, even among Catholics, in spite of the dead weight of the Biblical Commission. Theology does not cease to develop, notwithstanding some harsh braking. It is in this way that Catholics are at present elaborating a theology of the laity and a theology of labour, it is in this way that an outstanding theologian like Rahner has succeeded in making himself felt. But this religious research is still largely paralysed by an inquisitorial body like the "Holy" Office[2] and, above all, by the weight of tradition, which drags theology down like a leaden cope, to such an extent that the term "new theology" denotes something gravely pejorative and arouses the worst suspicions —as though today's tradition were not yesterday's progress! Now, to a biologist, an organism which does not progress is condemned to death. Teilhard, for his part, dreamed of a religious research which would not be confounded with free thinking, but which would comprise a wide margin of autonomy, in short, "experimental chapels" with a sincere programme of research, for example, into the enrichment which can be provided today by the countenance of God or our representation of Christ, research with everything that word implies in the way of trials, gropings, hesitations and second thoughts.

On 7 July 1954, the last time I saw him, Teilhard said to me something like this: "There is something in the Church which is illegitimate, out of line, but we have to pay for the fact that we have to belong to a phylum, where there is a process of co-spiritualization. Control is carried too far. The idea of research, of discovery, has not yet penetrated the Church of God because of the mistaken idea that Revelation is a closed circle. It is true that there has been some progress in historical criticism. I dream of an age in which there will be among the higher committees of the Church not only a Holy Office to whittle down, but a committee to study new ideas. It may come about in two or three generations. The idea of religious discovery has failed to penetrate, because of a mistaken idea of revelation." And in his paper on *Recherche, Travail et Ador-*

[1] ÉCRITS DU TEMPS DE LA GUERRE, Grasset, 1965, pp. 81–82. On this point see also p. 19 above. Eds.

[2] It has just, at long last, been reformed. (1966.)

ation, the second section of which is called 'Le conflit Religion-Science et sa solution', Teilhard observes: "In our days, by the force of events, a Christian can absolutely no longer give himself up sincerely to Research (and therefore cannot line up on equal terms with his non-Christian colleagues) without sharing in the fundamental vision which animates that Research:—that is to say, without first determining the conflict which exists in his innermost self, in nine cases out of ten, between the values of the traditional evangelical Above and the new human Ahead. Therefore, to tell a religious to practise the Sciences without allowing him, at the same time, to rethink the whole of his religious vision, is certainly (. . .) setting him an impossible task—and condemning him in advance to mediocre results, in a divided inner life."[1]

Not only does science involve a spirit which is bound to inform every mental approach, but it stimulates an overall vision of the universe, the evolutionist vision in cosmogenesis, which has very considerable repercussions on theology. As Teilhard noted on 24 October 1947:

"Science does not define a theology, but
(i) it excludes certain (intrusive) types

(a) of divine action
(b) of limited representations

(ii) it imposes certain dimensions."

The outstanding event which is taking place on the face of the Earth is our gradual realization that the world is on the move. On the whole, men had the idea that they were living in a pre-arranged system (static or cyclic) in which they had their allotted place. Now, it is this

---

[1] Cf. D. Dubarle, POUR UN DIALOGUE AVEC LE MARXISME, Paris, Ed. du Cerf, 1964, p. 33: "The believing intelligence must adopt not only what scientific conceptions tell us materially about reality, but also, in practice, an internal scientific spirit, a kind of instinctive, experienced, philosophy, which is implicit in science and which, moreover, it knows very well how to make explicit whenever necessary. This spirit, this philosophy, cannot be dissociated from the knowledge proposed by science without bypassing a capital part of its teaching (. . .). This is perhaps what religion is most blamed for not recognizing!" Cf. A. N. Whitehead, "Science has suggested a cosmology. And to suggest a cosmology is to suggest a religion." RELIGION IN THE MAKING, cited by N. M. Wildiers in LIVRES DE FRANCE, Paris, April 1966, p.10.

system which is beginning to move in the direction of organization. All this is heavy with consequence. What happens, in effect, in a world which is becoming organic, or rather, whose organic character is being discovered by the human mind? The philosophical overtones are numerous. I select one: the relations between mind and matter are changing. In a (static) perspective in cosmos, mind and matter constitute two categories, designating two things in juxtaposition. Between them there is no bridge. This is a fundamental dualism, a reified matter faced with a reified mind. In cosmogenesis of the convergent type, that is to say, where the universe is tending to concentrate and interiorize itself, mind is a function of the arrangement of matter. The relationship between the two elements is comparable to that between two variables of the same function. For mind to appear, there must be arranged matter. This is satisfactory to the mind; matter and mind are only two facets or two phases of the same reality. If we want more mind, we must have greater arrangement of matter.

This is not materialism. In a state of cosmos (in static perspectives), for the materialists, mind issues from matter, but when we adopt the point of view of cosmogenesis, there is nothing to stop us from admitting that the conscious superstructure is based on the material infrastructure. Materialism, in cosmogenesis, consists in affirming that the system *falls into equilibrium* on matter, while for those who take the mental side, it is the mentalized part, the mental summation, which remains. The important part is the end.

Now, these perspectives mean that major corrections must be made in the traditional accounts of the relation between mind and body, and of death as the separation between the two. As Dr. Paul Chauchard has very well said in his book NOTRE CORPS CE MYSTÈRE:[1] "It is a pity that, in the expression of religious verities and, for example, in the Catechism, the vocabulary of the Church is often denatured by that too Cartesian expression in which a body is presented as united with a soul. False problems thus arise with regard to the relations between science and faith, and the essential agreement disappears in the inadequacies of language."[2]

[1] Paris, Beauchesne, 1962, p. 168.
[2] Cf. G. Crespy, DE LA SCIENCE À LA THÉOLOGIE. ESSAI SUR TEILHARD DE CHARDIN Neuchâtel, Delachaux et Niestlé, 1965, p. 48: "A man *composite* of body and soul, flesh and spirit, is not only a paradoxical being, he is an *impossible* being."

Jean Guitton, in LE PROBLÈME DE JÉSUS,[1] had already written more forcibly: "(. . .) the Christian religion, correctly understood, does not teach the survival of the soul, or even the 'immortality of the soul', but the *reintegration* of that concrete man, commonly called the *flesh*. This amounts to saying (when the word is cleansed of popular images or concepts linked with ancient physics) that the present life of man will be transmuted into life of a higher order, in which no element of this life will be *annihilated* but in which each of them will be *sublimated*. A phrase in a liturgical chant, applied to the dead, says this soberly: *Vita mutatur, non tollitur*. Life undergoes a mutation, but is not taken away. This *mutation without ablation* is perhaps what is called resurrection."

Another consequence: in our human eyes, the face of God is changing, God is Christifying himself and becoming more immanent. In effect, man's accession to the vision in cosmogenesis leads to enlargements and embellishments in the vision of God. In cosmos, in a static vision of the universe, the element behaves like a small piece in a mosaic, where juxtaposition reigns. The idea of a creation exclusively *ex nihilo*, however obscure it may be, is in harmony with this vision in cosmos. On the other hand, in a vision in cosmogenesis, we see a world in which duration is the natural dimension of divine creation, a world which is groping, which is striving to unite, to arrive at constantly higher syntheses, from the megamolecule to man, from man to planetized mankind. Now, union, like the dough which cannot rise without ferment, requires a binding force, an internal factor of unification. Thus, the God of cosmos is the worker who acts efficaciously, whose deeds are extrinsic, so that the effects are produced outside himself and have nothing of their author but a distant imprint. On the other hand, if we look for the conditions of a God of convergent cosmogenesis, we find that the Creator is bound to act as an internal animating principle, by a force of animation, *interior intimo meo*, in St. Augustine's words. He acts not so much as a workman, but as a force of evolution. A ready-made world (static) *ipso facto* detaches itself from its creator. A world in the making, that is to say, in the process of unification, on the contrary, is no more able than an unborn child to detach itself from its creator, from the evolutionary and unifying principle which is giving it birth.[2]

[1] Paris, Aubier (Ed. Montaigne), Vol. II. 1953, p. 125.
[2] Cf. G. Crespy, DE LA SCIENCE À LA THÉOLOGIE. ESSAI SUR TEILHARD DE CHARDIN, Neuchâtel, Delachaux et Niestlé, 1965, p. 22: "Things are no

E

Naturally, we repeat, positive science has nothing to do with the mystery of death or that of divine creation. The scientist has nothing to say about creation, a metaphysical dimension which totally escapes him, and confines himself to recording phenomenal emergences, that is to say the appearance of increasingly autonomous, complexified, centred and interiorized systems. As for death, the biologist contents himself with trying to define, not without difficulty, the characteristics of physiological death, from apparent death to absolute death, and teaches us nothing about personal eschatology. Naturally, this vision in cosmogenesis is not, in the strict sense, a scientific cosmology, it is a phenomenology (a dialectic of evolution), that is to say, the first stage in Teilhard's philosophy, but this phenomenology remains none the less closely linked with science, it remains a synthetic and regulatory unitary ideal of science. This vision in cosmogenesis would not be possible without a sound scientific substructure. And this is a fact of the utmost importance. Not only does science, in the strict sense, pose imperious and indiscreet questions for the theologian—the Thomist theologian, Charles, a friend of Teilhard, felt himself obliged to carry out pre-historic diggings in Belgium—but theology also loses that kind of pre-eminence which was the source of a secret pride for very many theologians. It is true that it remains the science of the sacred, or more accurately, of the revealed, it preserves its own technique and methods, but Teilhard, as it were, restores it and embodies it in a unitary vision of the world. This is exactly the opposite position from that of Heidegger who remains the partisan of splendid (and fatal) isolation: "Only those epochs which themselves no longer really believe in the true greatness of the task of theology, arrive at the pernicious idea that a theology has something to gain from a purported revitalization with

longer at all the same if the world is in movement. It is, in effect, no longer a question of reflecting solely upon what may have happened at an original moment, but of discovering whether there is a *direction* pervading the movement of the world, if the 'world' is borne by a finality expressed through its moving stuff. God, in this perspective, can no longer be regarded as the necessary Being, the external cause of reality, and we must make up our minds to look upon him as the *direction* of reality, *in proportion as reality deploys itself. If the world is movement, then God is history*, or at least God can no longer be thought of as immobile, eternally frozen in his Being, but must be regarded as linked in some manner with the movement of the world."

the aid of philosophy."[1] In short, Teilhard restores theology to its place. Wolf, Kant's master, around 1730, already thought it necessary to change the traditional order, theology governing cosmology, cosmology governing anthropology. Theology and cosmology had to be brought back into rank and placed on an equality with anthropology. Wolf therefore introduced at the head a general metaphysics (the study of principles).

Another humiliation for theology: it finds itself secretly placed in the wake of science, or, to use more indulgent language, theology must remain attentive to the contributions of science in progressively making explicit the data of Revelation which, received by men who could only know and speak according to their times, mixed the chaff and the grain. Henceforward, it has become impossible for the theologian to speculate with his own methods and his own techniques without possessing a sound scientific knowledge and culture. It is true that theology does not depend on this or that specific discovery of detail, although moral theology remains closely linked to biology, but theology as a whole cannot fail to take account of the image of the universe elaborated by modern science, whose spiritual repercussions have proved to be incalculable. Without falling into scientism (science is not the only source of knowledge), we are living in the age of science, and one of the reasons for Teilhard's prestige is that he constantly talks the language of science, even in a spiritual work like LE MILIEU DIVIN, as the very title suggests.

But even this is not yet the most important point. In demonstrating that traditional theology is linked to a vision in cosmos, and that vision in cosmogenesis demands another theology, Teilhard, by that very fact alone, has reopened the question of the basic concepts of theology. Since Kant, no metaphysics is possible without a prior critique of knowledge; Teilhard, who was able to discover, by scientific synthesis, the unity of the creative design, at the same time as the direction in which it unfolds, is to some extent, as it were, the Kant of theology. Since Teilhard, theologians will always be bound to criticize their categories. It is easy to see the great importance of science, through its direct and, above all, through its indirect, consequences.

. . . So far we have been pleased to follow an easy line of thought, and a carping spirit might find that faith has rather lost face. Nothing

[1] Cited by J. Mouroux, LE MYSTÈRE DES TEMPS, Paris, Aubier, 1962, p. 9.

of the sort, and we now approach the most delicate part of our subject, which calls for a noticeably more intense intellectual effort.

Let us start with two witnesses. In Peking, when Teilhard came to know the American sculptor, Lucile Swan, he told her that science led to religion,[1] and these words remained graven in the artist's memory. Another witness is the German–American geologist and palaeontologist, Helmut de Terra, who tells us that when Teilhard examined a fossil or a stone (and he possessed a rare gift of observation) he seemed to see through it and beyond it, as though possessed by an imperious vision, by an intuition which made all things transparent.

One might be tempted to maintain that faith enlightened Teilhard in all his acts, and that his design is theological from start to finish. Teilhard's phenomenology, like that of Husserl, is preoccupied by the search for meaning. In the strict sense, the search for meaning is alien to positive science, which limits itself to establishing laws, to correctly linking cause and effect. Now, to the *homo religiosus*, the man of faith, it is quite evident that the world is oriented towards a certain consummation. The religious vision is eschatological. History is the act of God through men. Furthermore, if Teilhard had not, from his earliest childhood, learned to love Jesus Christ, would he have found Christ Omega as the motive force of evolution? One meets unbelievers who sincerely adhere to that vision of world history presented by LE PHÉNOMÈNE HUMAIN, but refuse to make the *saltus mortalis*, to confer on Omega the predicates of the absolute, to recognize in it the "natural" face of Christ. "You would not be seeking me, if you had not found me" says Pascal's Christ. Teilhard, from the outset, knew where he would end up, though ignorant of the avenues through which he would travel.

Considerations of this kind are not false, but we must confess that they are profoundly unsatisfying. In the first place, there is nothing specifically Teilhardian about the search for meaning, since classical phenomenology along the lines of Husserl is devoted to the same operation. Thinking like that of Hegel, with the fundamental theme of "God is dead", presents itself as resolutely finalistic. Moreover, it would singularly diminish the force of Teilhard's thinking. It is true that Teilhard had the soul of an apostle, he felt himself to be a missionary

---

[1] In expressing himself thus, Teilhard was in nowise lapsing into concordism. He simply meant that the spiritual mainspring of scientific research is of a religious nature.

in his soul, he had conceived the immense ambition of reconquering the modern world for Christ. It is true that he never lost faith in the Church, though he passed through spiritual tempests. But this faith in the Church changes nothing in the extreme sincerity, the absolute integrity, of his spiritual adventure, since Teilhard allowed himself to be led to the uttermost end of his thought. Those who knew him saw it clearly: when you asked him about a difficult point, he started absolutely from scratch, so that you wondered, with some surprise, whether it was really a Jesuit priest who was talking to you. Teilhard's intellectual adventure, which never failed to be true to itself, might, in the extreme case, have turned out badly. The threads might have snapped. In fact, it turned out well, but Teilhard, by a very rare gift, was able to sympathize fundamentally with the uncertainties of the Gentiles, and especially with the shifting spirits outside, the displaced persons of the faith, so numerous in our days. He was able to sympathize because he took his own risks in forcing himself to follow their line of thought, exposing his faith to the test of a rational phenomenology and dialectic.

But let us leave this line of thought, which seems dubious, ambiguous and not very convincing, and come to solid ideas. Just as faith calls for science (*fides quaerens intellectum*), so science, in Teilhard's eyes, has a mystical aura. It is not difficult to find in Teilhard, who was a genuine scientist, a self-forgetfulness, a disinterestedness, a constant need to go further, which could lead to heroism and total sacrifice. Teilhard's generosity as a scientist has become almost proverbial. How many memoirs he wrote for his young Chinese colleagues, from A to Z, and refused to sign! Now, how can the heroism of the researcher be explained, unless, underlying the need to know, there is a more profound driving force, of a religious nature? As Teilhard said, scientists feel obscurely that to know more is to be more, that a growth of consciousness also promotes an ontological growth. In other words, research, for the modern scientist, is no longer mere curiosity, the fruit of the *cupido cognoscendi*, it is a sacred function, a quasi-religious act. Without any confusion, the scientist tends to come near to the priest.

Teilhard, naturally, did not fall into the naiveties of the religion of science, he did not allow himself to be duped by the ersatz religion proposed by the Russians, but the fact nevertheless remains that in his eyes science reflected obscure religious needs which a higher psychoanalysis would have no difficulty in bringing into full light. Teilhard, in fact, wrote to his friend Abbé Gaudefroy: "For me, scientific research and mystic effort form a single complex power, which irresistibly insists upon propagating itself." The IMITATION scorned science by declaring that the four elements are the same everywhere and that, in consequence, this profane knowledge is of no interest. For Teilhard, on the contrary, whose spirituality lies, in some respects, at the antipodes of the IMITATION, research is rooted in adoration and in this, he is a true son of his Order, which numbers so many researchers and scientists.[1]

If, therefore, there is something religious in scientific research, if it desecrates the universe only to reconsecrate it *en bloc*, and if, therefore, it can lead to adoration, it is still possible to dismantle the existential mainsprings of science, or, if you like, to lay bare the roots and analyse the secret sap which nourishes the tree of science. A mathematician once confided in Teilhard: "I work in order not to die." No doubt he meant by that, that scientific research (like, indeed, the quest for beauty) is man's effort to immortalize himself, or rather to eternalize himself. As Nietzsche says, "man desires profound, profound eternity." Man aims at a κτῆμα εἰς ἀεί, an eternal good, the scientist as much as other men.

It is thus easy to see what are the intellectual origins of Teilhard's famous dialectic, of that existential dialectic which impels him to discover in point Omega not only a potential centre, but something real, something which makes irreversible, something self-sufficient, capable of bearing the weight of a world in evolution, of acting as a keystone to the universe. As Teilhard says, in his own language:[2] "(. . .) the evolutive God of science cannot, biologically, fulfil his function, at the head of Evolution, without being at the same time lovable and loving; in which case the traditional God of Christianity and the newly discovered God of evolution would become, in the last instance, one and the same reality in the human religious consciousness." On the one side, the scientist works in order not to die, in order to eternalize himself.

---

[1] The desire of the scientist, repeats Teilhard, is to "uncover the secret of the real, to find the source. The research of the scientist, however positivist he may profess himself, is coloured by and verges upon, or rather it is invisibly animated at heart by, a mystic hope." (Cited by E. Rideau, LA PENSÉE DU PÈRE TEILHARD DE CHARDIN, Paris, Ed. du Seuil, 2nd edition, 1965, p. 220, n. 116.)

[2] HISTORY OF THE CONFLICT BETWEEN RELIGION AND SCIENCE.

On the other side, the scientist is well aware that the human species and the Earth will die. The biologist seems to suggest that the human species will disappear like the others, the average life of species being some tens of millions of years. But the astrophysicist, for his part, contributes a certainty which can be regarded as irrefutable. It is known that the sun functions like a gigantic nuclear reactor, with the slow transformation of hydrogen into helium. We are even fairly familiar with the cycle of operations—the Bethe cycle, and, above all, the Critchfield cycle—and it has gradually become possible to specify, in the light of the knowledge acquired of solar physics, that the sun will last a few more thousand million years—five or six—after which there will be a cataclysm, a rupture of equilibrium, probably resulting in the death of the Earth by overheating, until the moment when the matter of the sun loses its superficial electrons and achieves the extraordinary density of the dwarf stars. At that moment mankind will long have been out of existence.

I am well aware that a Marxist would describe this vision of the end of the world as a fanciful dream, but, whatever he may say, modern man holds it for certain that not only civilizations, but the whole Noosphere are mortal. One of the reasons for the development of astronautics in Russia, in addition to the scientific, technical, military and political reasons which they have in common with the United States, is a religious motive. The object is to demonstrate to the vulgar crowd that neither God nor the angels are to be found in inter-sidereal space, to suggest that man is capable both of mounting into the heavens and of descending again, in other words of outdoing Jesus on Ascension Day, but above all, it is to guarantee the Noosphere a sort of immortality by inter-galactic emigration, in such a way that mankind can swarm and maintain itself indefinitely, thus sharing in the eternity of the cosmos. Objections of a biological nature are met by the prospects of hibernation, allowing human life to be suspended for the centuries needed to arrive at a new planetary system.[1]

[1] We do not make the Marxists say what they have never said. For them, it is matter which is eternal, and not mankind. But the second law of thermo-dynamics and the positive observations of astrophysics seem to suggest a growing entropization of the cosmos and a degeneration of stellar matter, which could be described (metaphorically) as the "death" of matter. In fact, these white dwarfs, with their atoms stripped of their electrons and of an incredible density, will be, after radiating their heat and their light, "dead" stars, and it is hard to see how they can come back

In the face of these Fourth Form daydreams—Thomas Tupper converted to the Gospel according to Karl Marx—it is, of course, impossible to assert that any particular undertaking is incapable of achievement, since it cannot be demonstrated *a priori* that anything at all is impossible, except a hippogriff, and it is the duty of a Christian to applaud and share in these marvels of human ingenuity. But we shall probably come up against limits of a biological nature, for man is, after all, no more than a cosmopolitan Primate, and his ubiquity is not indefinite. But, above all, one definitely senses in these grandiose anticipations (which cannot and should not be rejected out of hand) an attempt at diversion, in Pascal's meaning of the word, the gilded dream of a Noosphere, which imagines that in the National, or rather, Cosmic Sweepstake, it will win the first prize of immortality. The first prize of £100,000, £150,000 or £200,000 may well exist, but the first prize of the biological immortality of the Noosphere is a piece of science-fiction. The eschatology of mankind, of the Noosphere, forms one of the strong points of Teilhard's thought in particular, and of Christianity in general, and conversely, the great weakness of Marxism, even purged of the Thomas Tuppers who bring ridicule upon a great school of thought.

Thus Teilhard's philosophy is that of a scientist who questions himself about the existential mainsprings of science, but it is his Christian faith which impels him to question, for the whole of faith is a question put by man and answered by God, at least so far as man understands it. And this faith of Teilhard's, far from injuring his science, served to enlighten and prolong it, or, more accurately, to reveal its depths. The research worker is like a man imprisoned in a cave. The truth shines for him only as a narrow shaft of light; Teilhard has proved that this meagre luminous brush-stroke comes from God's great sun. In more abstract fashion, we can say with Teilhard: "(. . .) the traditional war between religion and science does not mean a final divorce, but it merely expresses one phase in the classical Hegelian scheme: Thesis (mediaeval Christianity: Love of God)—Antithesis (modern science, discovery of evolution)—Synthesis (a Christian religion of evolution, the love of

into the dynamic circuits of matter. Furthermore, without falling into the old ways of idealism and without in the least degree subscribing to donnish philosophy, the concept of a matter which was not the subject of a representation (human or divine) seems to me confused, contradictory and pre-critical.

Evolution: Omega)."[1] To sum up in a single phrase: Teilhard has given us a fundamental discovery, namely that faith alone comprises in the last resort the obscure intention of science, since the role of faith is to present a totalizing and integrating vision of the world.

Why did Teilhard succeed?—I revert to the broad fresco outlined in my introduction. The man of the Middle Ages, in spite of the tumultuous life of the Church, was, on the whole, a man fully reconciled, unified—rather like the primitive who lives in harmony with his tribe and with the cosmos.[2] With St. Thomas science and cosmology are embodied in a theological design: *Philosophia et cosmologia ancillae theologiae.* The spheres revolve harmoniously, sanctified by hosts of angels; in Dante topology and theology coincide exactly: at the centre of the Earth, the outcast souls, on Earth, living humanity, on trial, then the mountain of Purgatory and finally, Heaven, with the mystical rose of the elect revolving around the Holy Trinity. This admirable (and false) vision inspired the cathedrals, and those cathedrals of thought and poetry raised up by St. Thomas and Dante. But after the fifteenth century, theology in decadence, like a diseased stomach, fed on itself, and the Renaissance, discovering, through the fanciful dreams of astrobiology, the first foreshadowings of modern science, set off the conflict between science and faith, whose debates, discreet at first, have become as noisy and as vain as those of a parliamentary assembly.

Now, the great peaceable voice of Teilhard has practically stilled the tumult and created a new status.[3] How was he able to succeed? Reason is a gift of God, it is therefore of divine origin, and if God has given men reason, it is so that they may use it, in the sacred field as well as in others, which is in no way the world of the irrational, but a zone

[1] HISTORY OF THE CONFLICT BETWEEN RELIGION AND SCIENCE.

[2] But with this fundamental difference, that this universalist faith, sustained by a refined conceptualism, enabled him to overcome political and mental fragmentation.

[3] Don Aldo Locatelli in IL MESSAGIO SPIRITUALE DI TEILHARD DE CHARDIN, Milan, 1965, p. 103: "It is unquestionable that, however much one may criticize, discuss or weigh up the thought of Teilhard de Chardin, he will go down in history as the first man who tried to solve the problem of the relations between science and faith, not from a purely negative point of view, but positively, that is to say, by trying to construct a unitary synthesis with the data provided by the different types of knowledge." See J–O. Pinon, ". . . Teilhard wants to give a scientific dimension to religion and a religious dimension to science," in *Qu'est-ce que le teilhardisme?* LA PENSÉE ET LES HOMMES, Belgium, Feb.–March 1964, p. 225.

in which there reigns a certain type of intelligibility. It is true that God is not only the link of categories, essences and mathematical entities, he is the supreme living being. He is therefore trans-rational, as is suggested by the mystical concept of the *Deus absconditus*, the God of apophatic theology, but he is not irrational. Science therefore appears, as it were, as a natural revelation, a first revelation. How, therefore, is a conflict between natural revelation and supernatural revelation conceivable? God, on pain of denying himself—*ego sum veritas*—cannot contradict himself.[1] The reconciliation between reason and faith was therefore foreseeable from the very unity of God. To adopt the expressions of Jean-Marie Aubert:[2] "Complete unification between a scientific life and a life of belief seems to us not only possible, but demanded by the very nature of things."

A very simple example will illustrate this general statement. The Kerygma (the gospel message) teaches us the existence of a supernatural history, which is preparation, slow maturing and accomplishment. Paradoxically, the context of this Kerygma was a non-evolutionist vision of the world, and especially the vision of a human history in which nothing happens except the cyclical rise and fall of empires. Now, quite independently of this Kerygma, contemporary man has discovered evolution, that is to say that man is history and that "Time is the vector along which a World is organizing itself",[3] or in other words, that something really is happening which is a maturing of the spiritual. Christic maturing, spiritual maturing; who can fail to see that these two assertions, without originating from each other, reciprocally support each other? And who can fail to see that the second acts quite naturally as a prolegomenon to the first? There is not the slightest concordism about this, since neither of these two realities has been forced to make it fit the other or subordinate to the other. It is a simple "co-adaptation" in a unifying vision, and therefore much more satisfying to the mind, as satisfying as the integration of individual time,

---

[1] Cf. George B. Barbour, IN THE FIELD WITH TEILHARD DE CHARDIN, New York, Herder and Herder, 1965, p. 122: "There he reiterated his long-held belief in the unity of truth. In the final analysis he said, science and religion will converge as knowledge and understanding grow." (said in April 1948.) Newman had already said (*op. cit.* p. 446): "Truth cannot be contrary to truth."

[2] RECHERCHE SCIENTIFIQUE ET FOI CHRÉTIENNE, Paris, Fayard, 1962, p. 123.

[3] G. Crespy, DE LA SCIENCE À LA THÉOLOGIE, *op. cit.* p. 29.

from birth to death, in a vaster time, that of biological history, itself a simple prolongation of the history of the cosmos.

In the last analysis, was Teilhard content to hammer on an open door? What is original about his position?

In fact, he has discovered a new status of the relations between science and faith. He had to resolve the following antinomy: on the one hand, it is quite evident that rational thought is finally emancipated, a phenomenon parallel with the development of secularity (in the non-educational sense of the word) and of the laity. Reason has been desecrated. And not only has faith fallen back on positions not prepared in advance, but science, through the medium of vision in cosmogenesis, is continuing to pursue it with bayonets fixed, like the Chinese chased the Indians on the plains of Assam. This retreat, moreover, will one day stop, for reason, if it continues to take the offensive for too long, is in danger of the worst misadventures, those which lie in wait for an army which advances too fast, which fails to mop up behind it and whose lines of communication are stretched too far. The elastic withdrawals of faith have not been all loss, it has shed some useless baggage, and especially suspect mixtures with outdated cosmologies. Like every religion which sheds its trappings, that is to say, its paganism, it has purified itself, and in this purification, has found new strength, and once again become itself.

In short, science and faith remain autonomous and constitute two original modes of knowledge. On the other hand, man is ruled by a need for unity. *Homo duplex* does not exist. The generatrices of a cone all converge at the vertex. Dualism, born of analysis, avoids confusion of planes, telescoping, but it cannot have the last word, on pain of falling into a sort of Manichaeism or schizophrenia. Teilhard's solution seems absolutely satisfying, that of a dialogue, of a harmonious tension, a bipolarity which respects both powers. And thus I come to the master word, the keyword of my survey. Teilhard has discovered a new status between science and faith, which is much more than a gentlemen's agreement, which is convergence. All knowledge, specifies Teilhard, is fringed with faith, all religion constitutes the affective face of a Weltanschauung. Why? Because truth is one.

Everyone is familiar with Teilhard's fine phrase: "Everything which rises must converge." A faith which rises is purified of its dross—

clericalism, political and social compromises, more or less mythical representations, neo-Scholasticism, legalism, dolorism, intolerance, inquisitorial manias, diverse mystifications and alienations—to acquire the sense of critical research. Conversely, a science which rises disembarrasses itself of those Petticoat Lane philosophies, positivism, neo-positivism, physicalism, scientism, to become haloed with mysticism and to change into adoration. It is no longer a reciprocal *Noli me tangere*, it is a bilateral exchange of information, like two friendly nations which exchange military secrets and technicians. The oxygen circulates between the oratory and the laboratory in a well-conditioned flow. In the excellent words of Einstein:[1] "Science without religion is lame, religion without science is blind."

We close with the ironical remark of the Swiss biologist Agassiz, repeated by Lyell, the founder of modern geology and the friend and counsellor of Darwin: "Whenever a new and striking fact comes to light in science, people first of all say that it is not true, then that it is contrary to religion, and finally, that everybody knew it all along." The discovery of a status of convergence between science and faith seems to us a simple idea, but someone had to think of it.

---

[1] OUT OF MY LATER YEARS, New York, 1950, p. 29.

PART THREE

A Comment

by Roger Garaudy

Translated by A. O. Dyson

Any anxieties I might have had about the direction this conference would take were quieted from the first by Dr. Towers' words of introduction. He insisted that we were here to engage, not in some sort of cultic adulation, but rather in critical reflection upon Teilhard's thought.

This approach was confirmed by the contents of the first paper.[1] In discussing the origins of life, Fr. Elliott did not simply indulge in an exegesis of Teilhardian texts. On the contrary he took as his starting point the present state of scientific thought. In the period since Teilhard's death more decisive discoveries have been made in biology than were made over preceding centuries. But Fr. Elliott showed that recent developments in the sciences have not invalidated the line of enquiry which Teilhard suggested.

In this sphere Teilhard's merit does not lie in his having made new discoveries, but rather that he demonstrated to a Church which had for more than a century unprofitably persecuted or rejected Darwin, that the demands made by science were legitimate and that authentic faith had nothing to fear from them.

The three basic theses which emerged from Fr. Elliott's lecture are not in themselves new. A century ago, in his DIALECTIC OF NATURE, Karl Marx's colleague Engels formulated them quite clearly: 1. Life is nothing other than a certain degree of complexification and organization of matter. 2. Granted this thesis, Engels went on to define life in the following way, "It is the mode of existence of albuminoid substances" (what today we call proteins). 3. Life is born by spontaneous generation.

It does not detract from Teilhard's achievement that Engels had already given precise formulation to these three basic theses. Teilhard's merit lay in having gained access for these theses into a Church which had ceaselessly attacked them in the name of a misconceived spiritualism.

Dr. Fothergill approached the problem of orthogenesis[1] in the same

[1] See vol. 2 in this series. Eds.

spirit. He set about eliminating from this concept all mystical, finalistic and dogmatic elements. At the end of such a critical process, the hypothesis of orthogenesis emerges as a provisional expression of our confidence in the ultimate intelligibility of the universe. But it is one hypothesis among others. Thus: 1. This working hypothesis must *not* be elevated to the status of a dogma. 2. Nor must we say that even if this hypothesis is one day decisively refuted another will replace it along the same lines. For the over-all meaning of the world cannot be read off solely at the level of experimental science. We cannot make science say what faith alone can say. Nor may we return to the Hegelian myth of absolute knowledge, not even by projecting it into the future.

Meaning is not something which can be "read off"; it is not something which imposes itself upon us from outside like the law of gravity. It is rather a task which we have to accomplish and which requires of us an initiative, an act, a risk. It is a question of passing, by philosophical or religious means, from something which is *known* to an *action* which has to be performed.

Faith requires this wager, this affirmation that the world, history and life have a meaning and that Christ is the fulfilment of this meaning.

Fr. Elliott showed that Teilhard's thought did not *start* from the idea of evolution to pass, by successive generalizations, to the Christian vision of the world. Teilhard took the opposite course. As Fr. Elliott eloquently expressed it: Teilhard believed in the world in terms of man, and he believed in man in terms of his faith in Christ.

The final success of evolution depends on man's action and is guaranteed, in Teilhard, by faith in Christ. This is then an act of faith from which no scientific reading of the world can exempt us.

I think that Claude Cuénot, who possesses such an admirable knowledge of Teilhard's works, might, in his excellent lectures, have drawn attention to this governing thesis (which Teilhard developed in a lecture given at the École Normale Supérieure), namely that knowledge proceeds by a series of acts of faith—faith in the world, in the spirit, in Christ and in God.

This is of paramount importance, for faith necessarily implies a risk.

As a Marxist I believe, along with Teilhard, that the world and history have a meaning, and that our task and privilege consists in consecrating our life, and even our death, to the realization of this meaning. I wager all my human faith for this glorious future and for this meaning. And this is why, as an atheist, I take my stand with Teilhard against the false prophets of absurdity and despair. But I can never forget that it *is* an act of faith, even if science and history furnish me with stronger and stronger probabilities and presumptions in support of it.

The possibility is not excluded that at some point or other in scientific enquiry we should discover that the world as a whole is not going towards convergence but towards disintegration and death, and that our efforts result in failure. Fr. Teilhard himself did recognize the possibility that evolution might founder. In short, the battle is not won in advance, but he would be a poor soldier who would not agree to fight unless he had the prior certainty of victory.

The Christian then, like the Marxist, engages in this struggle with fear and trembling. It is always possible that God will abandon him and the world. Jesus himself, the Son of God, knew this authentic despair when he cried on the Cross, "My God, my God, why hast Thou forsaken me?" This is a true despair, not a spurious one based on the certainty that in the end all will be well. Similarly his death was not of the theatrical kind where, after the final curtain, the "corpses" get up again and take their bow.

I affirm unequivocally that, as an atheist, I find at this point of the Gospel narrative the most sublime image of man's greatness, when God himself, this riven God, groans in doubt and despair.

I should question the tenets of a Christian who could claim the benefit of Christ's act of faith, of his heroic wager, if he himself did not sometimes feel there was nothing to sustain him personally. I should question the tenets of a Christian whose faith does not pass along this path of a total doubt and a possible despair which acknowledge the possibility that the world has neither meaning nor intelligibility. And I should question the tenets of a Christian whose belief does not include this act of faith which requires from us that we give to the world its meaning and intelligibility. The honour of man and the honour of God are found only in the heart and the spirit of man, not in the cosmos.

It may seem odd for a Marxist to employ this kind of language. I do so because of my belief that it is perhaps at this point that we Marxists and Christians are closest to each other, and that it is Teilhard's chief merit to have helped us, on both sides, to be aware of this.

F

Thus I believe that science itself, where it is not confused with scientism or positivism, and where it is not limited merely to scientific knowledge gained up to now—I believe that science in growth, living scientific research, demands of us a similar wager and a similar act of faith. It is what Einstein called an act of faith in the ultimate intelligibility of the universe.

It is, in my view, at the level of such a critical theory of knowledge that the problems of the relationship between Christianity and science can be resolved, namely at the level not of knowledge itself but of a common faith in the intelligibility of the universe. Otherwise we shall always lapse into the different kinds of concordism of which Claude Cuénot gave examples in his lecture. They will be concordisms like that of the followers of Canon Lemaître who claimed that they could find in a scientific fact the verification of a certain religious doctrine of creation.

We must not make the same mistake with "orthogenesis", with "radial energy", or with any other Teilhardian notion. We must not let the trees prevent us from seeing the wood!

The exciting and fruitful feature of Teilhard's thought is also its basic feature. For him the progress of knowledge, the effectiveness of action, scientific knowledge and Christian love, all devolve upon the same act of faith. It is just such a totalising and integrating vision of the world which is affirmed when Teilhard speaks of science leading to religion. And it is this profound vision which makes Teilhard a master both of *joie de vivre* and of human unity.

It is our task to keep this message free from all dogmatism and sectarian spirit. Teilhard has kindled a marvellous fire. We should seek to preserve not the ashes but the flames.

PART FOUR

Teilhard de Chardin: A Tentative Summing-up

by Claude Cuénot

During the Whitsun holidays of 1962, on 9, 10 and 11 June, at the Cini Foundation in Venice, in the noble Benedictine setting of the island of San Giorgio Maggiore, an International Seminar on Pierre Teilhard de Chardin was held under the auspices of PAX ROMANA, *at which six papers were read, each of which was followed by cordial and closely reasoned discussion. Coming after Cerisy-la-Salle, Bruges, Nice, Paris (the Conference of French Catholic Intellectuals) and, above all, the annual Seminars arranged at Vézelay by the Association Teilhard de Chardin, this was a sort of final consecration. In France and Switzerland, Spain, Italy and Germany, all over Europe, doctoral theses on Teilhard de Chardin are being written and sustained. Publications of high quality are beginning to multiply, and new interpretations are accumulating. The time has now come when a few very tentative working assumptions can be suggested.*

I THE GENERAL IDEA OF THE 'SYSTEM': COSMOS AND COSMOGENESIS

The outstanding event which is taking place on the face of the Earth is our gradual realization that the world is on the move. On the whole, men had the idea that they were living in a prearranged system in which they had their allotted place. Now, it is this system which is beginning to move in the direction of organization. The macrocosm, like the microcosm, is on the move.

This transition from the concept of a prearranged world to the concept of a world in the process of arrangement is the transition from a vision in cosmos to a vision in cosmogenesis. What are the historic phases of this transition? Broadly speaking, its beginnings go quite a long way back, to the sixteenth and seventeenth centuries and the influence of Copernicus and Galileo. In truth, Galileo's feat of finally exploding the geocentric doctrine was as incomplete as it was decisive. In effect, he did not touch the Cosmos; by making the Sun a fixed star, he merely changed the axis of the system. But in doing so, he cut the ground from under the feet of the thinkers. By shifting the axis, he divorced the centre of geometrical movements (the Sun) from the centre of psychic life (the Earth). By introducing a dualism into the Cosmos, he exploded the concept of Cosmos, undermining the prestige of the vision of a hierarchy of interlocking spheres. Just as a caterpillar starts to spin a cocoon, so the old cosmos went into the melting-pot, ready to be recast. And the butterfly which emerges is the vision in cosmogenesis.

From this amorphous mass, a new order has reappeared at different points. Astronomy lags provisionally behind. Newton's concepts, inspired with genius as they were, could be applied to a cosmos. They constituted an admirable rationalization, but did not suggest the appearance of a new vision.

But, in 1755, a work appeared in Königsberg under the title, ALLGEMEINE NATURGESCHICHTE UND THEORIE DES HIMMELS, ODER VERSUCH VON DER VERFASSUNG UND DEM MECHANISCHEN URSPRUNGE DES GANZEN WELTGEBÄUDES, NACH NEWTONISCHEN GRUNDSÄTZEN ABGEHANDELT, the author of which was Immanuel Kant, which already foreshadowed the theories formulated by Laplace in the closing years of the eighteenth century and adumbrated a cosmogenesis (the nebula which transforms itself into a sun and planets . . .). But the main focal point was natural history, which is one of the centres to which the human vision clings. As long ago as 1759, the German Wolf, in his THEORY OF THE GENERATIONS, attacked the immutability of species.

It was natural history which brought us the vision of a certain biological evolution with which people have wrongly sought to identify the whole of evolution—Teilhard's thought is not that of panbiologism. Moreover, everyone knows that the nineteenth century was the century of history, the history of institutions, of religions, of dogmas. . . .

It is true that all this still remained dispersed. But now the whole of physics and astrophysics have entered into the perspective of a cosmogenesis. People talk of a history of matter, as they talk of the birth, life and death of stars. In the nineteenth century, physics was still a matter of pure mathematics. Today, physics has entered into history. It is true that even in the nineteenth century, one historic concept had gained ground, namely, that of entropy, rendering exchanges of energy irreversible. But nowadays, people talk currently of the evolution of matter, to which a major part of nuclear physics is devoted. Nowadays, everything is a unity, there are no longer many separate movements, but one great complicated movement of cosmogenesis. Evolution is no longer a hypothesis, but the whole condition of all thought, and this cosmogenesis is not a periodic movement but a movement of convergence. Beings tend to group themselves in increasingly complex and interconnected units, the complexity being marked by a special parameter: the more complexity increases, the more progress there is in arrangement and centration and the greater is the inner consciousness.

All this is heavy with consequence. First of all, what happens in a world which is becoming organic, or rather, whose organic character is being discovered by the human mind? In such a world, the relation between mind and matter is changing: the place of evil is explained; the situation of each of us is modified; the terminations of the world are better defined than in a state of cosmos.[1]

---

[1] Occasional passages in this essay appear elsewhere (e.g. the passage that follows, on p. 64). They are retained here for the sake of logic and balance within this essay. Eds.

The relations between mind and matter are changing.

In a (static) perspective in cosmos, mind and matter constitute two categories, designating two things in juxtaposition. Between them there is no bridge. This is a fundamental dualism, a reified matter faced with a reified mind. In cosmogenesis of the convergent type, mind is a function of the arrangement of matter. The relationship between the two elements is comparable to that between two variables of the same function. For mind to appear, there must be arranged matter. This is satisfactory to the mind; matter and mind are only two facets or two phases of the same reality. If we want more mind, we must have greater arrangement of matter. This is not materialism. In a state of cosmos, for the materialists, mind issues from matter, but when we adopt the point of view of cosmogenesis, there is nothing to stop us from admitting that the conscious superstructure is based on the material infrastructure. Materialism, in cosmogenesis, consists in affirming that the system *falls into equilibrium* on matter, while for those who take the mental side, it is the mentalized part, the mental summation, which remains. The important point is the end. Phenomenally, mind appears as a function of matter. But the important thing is to know whether it is the stable partner. Thus we see that everything takes on a different meaning.

In cosmogenesis we find perspectives which provide an intellectual solution to the problem of evil.

In cosmos, we do not know how evil can initially arrive, there must be a catastrophe or an accident, very difficult to interpret. It is quite different in a cosmogenesis of convergence: in a world in the process of arrangement, it is statistically inevitable that there should be dis-arrangements and lack of arrangement, or, in short, disorders. Evil is a by-product of evolution; when a rocket rises, it leaves a trail of smoke behind it. From the intellectual point of view, the problem of evil does not exist. As to the acceptance of evil, that is quite a different question; we may very well fail to be reconciled to the disorder of the universe. In truth, Christianity has taught us how to place a value on evil and redeem it. The disintegration which is the expression of evil can be brought back into use to speed up cosmogenesis, this short-coming can help the individual to find a principle for overcoming his egoism and giving more to the world.

The place of the element in the whole takes on an entirely different aspect.

In cosmos, the element behaves like a small piece in a mosaic, where juxtaposition rules. Each element is more or less interchangeable and limited in its outline. In cosmogenesis, for each of us, there is no way of finding a backward limit, since each of us is indefinitely conditioned. And forward, we continue, since our effects remain and develop in solidarity with the whole world. In reality, we are each literally coextensive with the whole universe, in an infinitesimal way. From the ontological point of view, we occupy the whole universe. Each of us is partially everything.

The vision in cosmogenesis throws light on the terminal form of the universe.

In cosmos, there is no reason for it to begin or end. On the other hand, in cosmogenesis, it is easy to understand that there may be irreversible thresholds, and, in cosmogenesis of convergence, we can conceive a limit to this process of arrangement. We can even try to define precisely some of the conditions which govern this term of convergence. In a cosmogenesis of convergence, we find mankind folding in upon itself and becoming centred. Now, what conditions can we define to make the movement possible? For mankind to converge upon itself it must have the desire to converge, it must feel the desire to converge, it must take an interest. But if there is to be a desire, there must be an open way ahead. Man, if he is to seek and to evolve, must recognize that evolution is not reversible. There must therefore be a summit, an open way, a centre of irreversibility—which are the "phenomenal" characteristics of a God. God is the condition for the excitation of mankind in the process of cosmogenesis. Man works in order not to die. A closed cosmogenesis would be stifling. To postulate the existence of a way out at the summit is to postulate the rationality of the world. The world would be contradictory, or in other words, absurd, if evolution become conscious of itself were to crumble into *taedium vitae*.

There we have a first set of philosophic consequences. Second set of consequences: the face of God is changing. God is Christifying himself and becoming more immanent. In effect, man's accession to the vision in cosmogenesis leads to enlargements and embellishments in the vision of God. The God of cosmos is the worker who acts efficaciously, whose deeds are extrinsic, so that the effects are produced outside himself and have nothing of their author but a distant imprint. On the other hand, if we look for the conditions of a God of convergent cosmogenesis, we find that the Creator is bound to act as an internal animating principle, by a force of animation. He acts not so much as a workman, but as a force of evolution. A ready-made world (static or cyclical) *ipso facto* detaches itself from its creator. A world in the making, that is to say in the process of unification, on the contrary, is no more able than an unborn child to detach itself from its creator, from the evolutionary and unifying principle which is giving it birth.

Thus, God must, in a certain fashion, enter into cosmogenesis. He will thus find himself partly immersed, incorporated in a system in the process of evolution, and therefore suffering, since there is no evolution without suffering. The God of cosmogenesis therefore has an element of the incarnate and of the redeemer, and therefore of the fellow-sufferer. Cosmogenesis seems to incline us towards a God who fairly closely resembles the Christian God, since the centre of convergence must be "within" and cosmogenesis invites us to Christify the God appropriate to it. It therefore seems to call upon the Christian God. But by a return shock, it will act upon our religious representations in such a way that the Christian God is bound to be enormously enlarged, and Christ constrained to be formidably extended since he can only supernaturalize the world by completing it. To complete it in him, he must first complete it in itself, since Christ is, at the same time, the principle of supernaturalization, and the ultra-humanizing principle of evolution. In short, cosmogenesis compels us to Christify the rational God and cosmify the traditional Christ.

The third and last set of consequences is the appearance of a certain new energy, a certain desire for cosmogenesis. In effect, we witness the appearance of a psychological force of a new type, the love of evolution. The universe, as it converges on the centre, becomes loving, and since it becomes loving, the world becomes lovable, so far as we regard it as being in the process of centration. By virtue of the accession of his mind to vision in cosmogenesis, man realizes that, in the movement in which he is involved, he becomes responsible and charged with cooperation. Furthermore, since the world reveals itself to him as lovable, man conceives the idea of uniting himself with the universe as the image of God. In sum, he becomes alive to his true function, and at the same time he discovers a special energy. The forces which we call the forces of love are the most powerful known to man. Limited first to the couple, to the family, to the group, this energy may transform itself into a generalized energy.

We therefore see a new mystique elaborating itself before our eyes. Throughout his thousands of years of life, man has felt himself torn between his upward aspirations towards "Heaven" and the terrestrial values of the Earth beneath, between the conquest of Heaven and the call to possess the Earth. Through cosmogenesis, a possible reconciliation becomes apparent between the abscissa OX (beneath) and the ordinate OY (above), *a via tertia*, OR, forward. For modern man, through the Christic diaphany of matter, through the ascent of cosmogenesis to meet the divine grace, the ancient passion for the divine can be synthesized with the ancient passion for the Earth. Far from accepting the idea that the Earth is cooling down, we can believe that it is taking fire and burning with a new mystic blaze.

II   ANGUISH

Externally, Teilhard's thought can be defined as a living dialectic, a half-way philosophy between the existential and the conceptual. Now, the concept of existence is linked with the concept of anguish. We therefore deem it essential to study anguish and evil in Teilhard.[1]

The problem is as follows: is Teilhard an ingenuous optimist with an inadequate knowledge of suffering, human anguish and the force of evil, who therefore left them out of his reckoning? Do we find in him a romantic breath of unreflecting hope, or a conceptual architecture which would absorb evil in a theodicy of the Leibnitz type? For us modern men, this breath of hope would be something unreflecting. Now Teilhard is neither such a romantic nor such an architect of an outdated philosophy. Jean Wahl has said, "Where there is no anguish, there is no philosophy of existence." Conversely, where there is anguish, there is something approaching the philosophies of existence. Teilhard is not an existentialist. But was not the existential present in him? Was there not a presence of existence and anguish? Now, if there is an evil

[1] In these pages we content ourselves with summarizing an admirable talk by Madeleine Barthélemy-Madaule at the Collège Philosophique, 44 rue de Rennes, Paris, on 11 December 1961, with the addition of a few personal reflections.

of anguish, there is an anguish of evil; anguish and evil are intimately bound up together, in the experience of life they are the same. But, if they are present they cannot be conjured away in favour of a conceptual–universal. They give on to the acuteness of reality. On the plane of experience of life, anguish is evidence comparable to the evidence of Descartes in the ascesis of doubt. Anguish is a travelled road towards being.

First of all, did Teilhard share in the wakening of human anxiety which is characteristic of the modern world? Did he experience the problem of salvation, or did the problem of knowledge overshadow the problem of salvation? So much for Teilhard the man. In other words, does he bear witness to anguish? If it is true that Pascal met Cartesian optimism (Descartes as the prophet of man, the master and possessor of nature) with a negation of the world, it can be said that Teilhard answers Pascal and accepts his challenge, Teilhard follows a living dialectic of which Pascal is one of the terms. His answer is a theme which supplements another theme. And not only does Teilhard answer Pascal, but he answers himself. In him there is perhaps a Pascal and a Descartes, a man who on the one side says "Yes" and, on the other, says that the world is nothing in comparison with the transcendent, who says "No" to a temporal and necessary success of the world. Teilhard has attempted a very difficult, ardent and living synthesis between two contradictory positions—a synthesis perpetually reconstructed and in evolution. He flouts contradictories, as Jankélevitch would say. The synthesis is there, the anguish is therefore not purely provocative, but dwells at the very heart of Teilhard's philosophy. Did he not write, in 1949, UN PHÉNOMÈNE DE CONTRE-ÉVOLUTION EN BIOLOGIE HUMAINE OU LA PEUR DE L'EXISTENCE (A phenomenon of counter-evolution in human biology, or the fear of existence)? And, according to Father Pierre Leroy, Teilhard experienced terrible moments of anguish, the anguish of one who has seen, for it is difficult to bear a certain amplitude of vision.

But, if anguish is to reach the metaphysical plane, it must detach us from the illusory and lead us to the authentic. Did Teilhard experience that anguish? Yes, because that anguish led him to the *interior intimo meo*, to that Other which is more intimate to us than ourselves. There is a fine passage in LE MILIEU DIVIN[1] which shows Teilhard descending to the depths of himself and arriving at a bottomless abyss

[1] Ed. du Seuil, p. 75. English translation p. 54.

whence he discovers new abysses. Teilhard is then very near to Pascal, with this unlikelihood of finding himself existing in the midst of a successful world. He gives the response to Pascal's theme (in the complementary and musical sense of the word "response"). The fundamental anguish is, of course, that of death.[1] Naturally, it is not rationally that anguish leads us to refuge in God. For Teilhard, the horror, if we will it, is God, it is at the heart of the horror that the transfiguration-transformation of the dark into light takes place on the instant.

Another question; how does anguish stand in Teilhard's ontology? Has it been genuinely integrated into the heart of that vision? For Teilhard, the being is in evolution; he is therefore incomplete and precarious, he is completed by a process which Teilhard has unveiled by reflections drawn from every domain. The sole Vector of the world is the law of complexity-consciousness under which the world is increasingly centring itself and constitutes a tier of ever more powerful centres, converging on a single point ahead. Thus, we achieve a vision of the creative union of being, in the process of creative union. Are we not then in danger of falling into a kind of monism? No, for two reasons. In the first place, this union is creative at each level of emergence. There is a contingency, a happening, at each level— prepared, but not determined. The being struggles to unify the multitude. Then, in this "struggle" of the One against the Many, two ontological principles are revealed. The unifying factor can only be some principle other than the Many, although there is only one single phenomenal movement, and the dualism is not reflected at the beginning of the world only. At every instant, the Many is a brake. At all levels there is a return to latent multiplicity. As we have seen, for Teilhard there is no question of mind and matter. In his eyes there is mind-matter, matter in the process of spiritualization. Even on the spiritual plane, the Many is there. Nothing is static, final. But in a world looked at in this way, it is obvious that anguish is well founded. Being is torn between the appeal of the One and an ever-threatening Multiplicity. The sundering is already in the being, the being is crucified. Crucifixion is in the origins. Our world is incomplete, precarious, constantly menaced.

[1] LE MILIEU DIVIN includes many passages on death. Cf. French text, pp. 84 and 93, English translation, 61, 68. See also p. 172, French, p. 128 English, the very fine passage with overtones of Pascal and existentialism: "(. . .) on certain days the world seems a terrifying thing: huge, blind and brutal." *et seq.*

In sum, Teilhard has replied to Pascal by the convergence of time
and evolutive centration, his optimism consists in regarding man as
the spearhead of evolution. At the same time that he discovers anguish,
therefore, he discovers hope. The human soul has the double essence
of anguish and hope. Teilhard has assumed them both.

We have spoken of man: Teilhard felt how much his emergence
reflected this precariousness of the world. In LA LUTTE CONTRE LA
MULTITUDE (1917),[1] he wrote:

"The manyness of the flesh, the dualism of human nature, the
very complexity of the soul, in which the dust of a scarcely consoli-
dated world vibrates and trembles in the forefront: the misery of the
universal Many within us.

". . . And Misery, also, of the universal Many around us!

"(. . .) we fancy we can still hear the plaints of our small, selfish
being, begging for a little extra happiness.

"In reality *that which groans within us is greater than ourselves*. The
voice we hear, then, is that of the unique Soul of future times, weeping
within us for its Manyness. And it is the breath of this infant soul,
again, which passes in us in the fundamental, obstinate, incurable
desire for total union, by which all poetry, all pantheism, all sanctity
vibrates (. . .) Nothingness, Suffering, Sin—ontological Evil, Evil felt,
moral Evil—*three aspects of the same evil principle*, infinitely slow to
conquer, constantly reborn: Manyness."

Thus, anguish reveals in us something finer and greater than
ourselves. The troubling desire is planted within us like a vocation.
If our soul is full of anguish, it is because it is a prey to the Many,
because it is destined for terrifying metamorphoses. We must wait
until the centre which we are enters into higher syntheses, until we are
integrated and intensified in our person. This is the apparent contradiction of the future. On the one side we find the temporal synthesis of
socialization, which is both the sacrifice and the exaltation of the person,
and, on the other, by death, the religious formation of the Mystical
Body. On both sides, death and resurrection. The emergence of man is
at the same time the coming to being of the crisis of anguish—the fear
of not being heard (the evil of space-time, the immensity, opacity and

[1] In ÉCRITS DU TEMPS DE LA GUERRE, Paris, Grasset, 1965, pp. 118, 119 and
122.

aggressive impersonality of the social world), the fear of no longer being able to move (the evil of starting off), the fear of being hemmed in (the evil of the blind alley, the radical, dimensional impossibility of our experience escaping from time and space). To be shut in, cosmically, all together, in the universe; to be shut in atomically, that is to say, individually, each for himself, within ourselves, that is therefore the drama of man's estate. The evil of loneliness and anguish in a universe which we have not yet succeeded in fully understanding or in fathoming what it wants of us.

Man is a perfect and punctiform centre, but liberty and lucidity carry anguish to the extreme. From liberty we learn that everything depends on us. Teilhard has been called a philosopher of nature. This is true, but at the moment when the human being springs up, there is a reversal. It is consciousness which takes charge of nature. We commit not only ourselves, but the whole world, whence arises an acute crisis. The world might well deny itself, when it recognizes itself through reflection, and then the world would die. Teilhard summons men to the great option. Either the world will be promoted by liberty or it will die. Here, then, is the fundamental anguish of being. The world may be absurd (perhaps Teilhard envisaged this), faith may be a mirage. But, up to the end, Teilhard assembled a body of evidence which enabled him to master the vertigo of nothingness. Up to the end, he overcame the temptation of the absurd, the temptation of disgust. Thus, anguish is bound up with the essence of contemporary man and Teilhard does honour to anguish.

From this, consequences can be drawn for the problem of evil. In truth, this problem, as seen by Teilhard, deserves to be treated with the utmost precaution and the utmost precision. We shall confine ourselves to treating it with reference to the problem of anguish. Teilhard himself has said that it was a contradiction of his whole outlook to see no evil. It issues at every pore, the world would be a trickery if there were no evil. It must indeed be said that Teilhard saw evil *more* than it has ever been seen before, because of the exceptional quality of his sensitivity, the dimension of his vision, the acuteness of his sight, his passion for the essential Good (the will of God) and for the success of the world loved by him and by God. Evil (which is opposition to God's loving will) was hated by Teilhard in the measure of his passion for the divine will, and the evolution of responsibility in the world is in relation to the universal and progressive dimension of evil (as of the good to which evil is opposed). Born with intelligence, the temptation to revolt must constantly vary and grow with it.

But if evil can hold a place in the heart of anguish, it is because it is a value bound up with human freedom. According to Jean Wahl there is a contradiction between anguish and a philosophy of being. In Teilhard there is certainly a philosophy of the fullness of being, there is a requirement of fullness. When man springs up, he becomes the legislator of nature, he is entrusted with the future of being, he is responsible for the greater fullness of being, for inventing the being that is to come. By inventing values, man invents being. But this is exactly why evil fills such a large place, because it is bound up with human freedom, because it is a value. Ontological evil is founded on the Many. This is not positively evil, but because it is worked upon by the One, it necessarily leads to the emergence of evil. In the gropings towards unification, needs must that evil comes—*necessarium est ut scandala eveniant*. When we come to human error, to the level of moral evil, of conscious evil, the root of the error proves to strike very deep. Since he is the first centred being, man is greatly tempted to regard himself as the ultimate centre! For the first time, with man, a punctiform centre appears. What a temptation to regard oneself as an end, by a misguided synthesis, by a false unity! Here is root enough for evil.

Let us wind up these reflections on anguish. When we look at this train of thought, the complexity of these perspectives transcends all criticism. To enter into a dialogue with a thinker, unfair criticism must be transcended. What we find in Teilhard is not a radical anguish, but an anguish which is one of the terms of an ardent dialectic whose other term is hope, since, faced with the pain of evolution or cosmic anguish, Teilhard's whole thought is aimed at overcoming fear, at justifying existential confidence:

"The power of reflection introduces man into a higher and privileged compartment of things (dynamic neo-anthropocentrism); the power of co-reflection gives man the power to make a fresh start with evolution in an entirely new domain (the universe in convergence); a critical point of ultra-reflection takes shape at the term of the human rebound as a door open on the irreversible."

The mouth of the tunnel is not walled up, it gives on to the light, the sunlight of the absolute. With dramatic optimism, Teilhard heroically kept both ends up to the last. The world is not wholly dark, courage lies in holding both ends of the chain, thesis and antithesis, and doggedly seeking the synthesis which is to be found only in Jesus, crucified and transfigured. With Teilhard anguish is not, as it is with Kierkegaard, a leap from the finite into the infinite, it is the willingness to traverse the finite to the very end, the acceptance of one's presence in the world with all the terrible impotence of man. We are travellers between an origin and a term which we know not. Man is terrifyingly potent and impotent. Teilhard's anguish is the willingness to traverse the world. To Pascal, Jesus is in agony until the end of the world, to Teilhard the human fact is more like the stations of the cross than an idyll.

III   PHENOMENOLOGY

In sum, it is not hard to discover in Teilhard a surmounted existentialism; now, it is common knowledge that the existentialists, and especially Sartre, have borrowed from Husserl a method known as phenomenology. Teilhard, too, though in a highly original fashion, is a phenomenologist. He seeks to reach an understanding of man by considering him in his "milieu" or environment, and he desires to abstract nothing, to drop nothing from this environment of space and time.[1] He takes the whole cosmos, and his opus is essentially a universal history, going beyond historical periods.

We propose to bring out the logic of this opus and follow its course. We shall divide our comments into five parts, five successive stages, (1) the remote past, (2) the more recent past, (3) the present, (4) the near future, (5) the distant future. There are thus five stages in the history of the universe. Their sweep is continuous, but they are not episodes of equivalent value, they are the acts of a drama, the phases of an organic development, each phase calling for a particular cast of thought.

PHASE I: THE REMOTE PAST. The study of this past teaches us that the universe is evolving. Not only did life spring up gradually, but the earth has its origin in a system, the earth has its history. This history

[1] From this point onwards we summarize, with some modifications and additions, an admirable talk by Francis Elliott at the Conference of French Catholic Intellectuals on 29 October 1960.

of life and of the earth is an ascending phenomenon, and evolution takes the form of a recurrent growth.

(a) It is a growth. Here three concepts must be brought into play, multiplication, progression and irreversibility. There is multiplication: Teilhard has recognized that in nature accumulation tends to involve complexification. When matter accumulates, it concentrates, if the circumstances are favourable, and this concentration involves complexification. This "con-centration" includes "centration". In effect, matter, in complexifying, acquires a centre. Matter has a spontaneous tendency towards the heterogeneous and displays an order. The fundamental law is that of ascending evolution. Thus, this multiplication entails an organization.

Evolution is a progressive growth. Life develops in the direction of the autonomy of the individual; it is a progress towards greater independence from the external environment, it terminates in what are called "closed systems", and is therefore endowed with a certain autonomy.

This growth constitutes an irreversible progress. Nature never goes back on itself. A mammal, such as the whale, may again become aquatic, but it remains a mammal, and its adaptations remain purely external. This proves the value of time. The concept of reversibility is purely academic.

(b) Evolution is a recurrent growth, or in other words it passes through phases which repeat themselves at different levels and in different fashion; phases of divergence, of convergence, of emergence. Let us take a series of examples.

Let us look first at matter at its elemental level. The swarming of elemental particles, electrons, protons, neutrons, neutrinos, mesons, present different forms of the existence of matter. This is the phase of the divergence of matter. But these particles converge and terminate in a relatively stable system, the atom, which is already an emergence, that is to say something new, since it forms a unit quite different from a simple accumulation.

At the level of the atom, matter has diverged again by diffraction into the atoms of Mendeleef's table. But convergence comes into play again. These atoms have converged into more or less stable groups (the chemical radicals) terminating in the privileged compounds of molecules, which in turn represent an emergence.

The molecules, at their level, again constitute a divergence, since

G

their types are extremely varied. But they have converged by combining together and resulting in macro-molecular compounds, among which one special type can be distinguished, the molecule of protein, especially of complex protein, a substance with the power of self-reproduction (the virus, which reproduces itself in a biological environment).

The proteins, in turn, form a vast diverging universe, but these macro-molecules have converged to give birth to the cell. In truth we do not yet know how the cell issued from the protoplasm (undifferentiated living matter) and if it was produced by septation. In any event, it represents a new emergence.

The cell, in its turn, has diverged. First, we find single-cell organisms, such as the yeasts, of which there are many varieties. But these single cells have converged, first forming aggregates, the vestiges of which are represented by the colonizing animals, groups of different cells, living together, but capable of leading a separate existence. Next, the metazoa emerged from this intermediate form of convergence. The cell remains the basic unit, but the cells are differentiated, they result in differentiated organs, and therefore in the emergence of a higher unit.

Thus, the history of the universe is a recurrent growth, which passes through different phases, different levels. One might be tempted to adopt the image of the spiral, except that it is too linear. From level to level there is continuity plus total difference. Quantum physics raised the question whether the properties of molecules could not be calculated from their component atoms. It has partially succeeded. It will perhaps be more and more successful. But the emergence remains something quite new, new in relation to the elements from which it has sprung, new in relation to the novelty of the preceding emergence. The new is truly new. As Bergson says, evolution is creative (creation being the contribution of an unforeseeable novelty). In truth "creative evolution" is a tautology and we should not allow ourselves to be misled by its etymology ("development out of . . ."). Evolution is not confined to bringing out the implicit (the appearance of latent properties suddenly revealed by the crossing of a threshold, such as the "within" of things, the psychic) it is at every level a creative synthesis, an emergence.

PHASE II: THE MORE RECENT PAST: The assertion that man is the culmination of evolution is founded on a very positive conception of world history: (a) man is the culmination from the point of view of natural history. He is the last comer, the organism best dispersed over the globe, the most cosmopolitan, as well as being morphologically the least specialized organism, and finally, he is the being with the most retarded development, thus leaving vast possibilities of education. (b) Man is the culmination from the point of view of complexity, especially in his nervous system and his brain. In man's cerebral cortex alone there are about fourteen thousand million neurons (nerve cells) which, with their extensions, form an inextricable lattice-work. What figures should we reach if we could number all these connexions? (c) Man is the culmination through his consciousness. Vegetables are dominated by the functions of assimilation, animals by their motor functions which enable them to go in search of food. Man is dominated by a third function, that of information (in the cybernetic meaning of the word). Naturally, this is already found in animals, but in man this function of information has become a specialty, he is capable of information about information, in short, he possesses a reflecting consciousness. And it is there that man reaches that summit of independence witnessed by the cosmonauts.

PHASE III: THE PRESENT: Man is the summit of evolution, but the laws of recurrent growth can be applied to him, indicating to us that mankind is passing through a particular phase of human planetization. (a) It is easy to talk of human divergence, of the spontaneous tendency to divergence; examples are so abundant that there is no need to stress them—the divergence of language, the balkanization of French-speaking Africa, and so forth. (b) Convergence: the accumulation of men has almost necessarily united them, first, on the zoological plane (the maintenance of the cross-fertility of races), then on the reflexive plane (the existence of vital communities such as the great capitals, which alone make certain forms of culture possible). This convergence operates in necessary fashion, it contains an element of necessity. (c) Emergence: the association of men is coming about gradually on a world-wide scale, and we are witnessing the commencement of a new emergence, planetization, the tendency to join together in a single community. Its various aspects are space exploration, the development of means of communication, economic, technical, industrial and cultural[1] interdependence, and, finally, war. In sum, planetization is the convergence of all men in a new unit.

[1] The theatre is only possible in a large town, and the cinema, above all, is an international art-form, which calls for an international public.

PHASE IV: THE NEAR FUTURE, OR THE TENSION OF THE PRESENT ON THE FUTURE: The best words to describe this near future are the rebound of evolution. From accumulation we move on to concentration: mankind, impelled to planetization, must now interiorize this planetization, since the appearance of consciousness marks a genuine watershed in world history, a transformation such that matter begins to escape from itself. Man becomes responsible for the pursuit of evolution. It is not enough for him to accept it passively, he must recognize that this evolution is well founded and must have the will to complete it, and therefore must love and accept it.

So far we have remained within the field of science, in the broad sense of the exact observation of what is going on around us. In this fourth phase we are still in the same domain, since this near future is already present in us in embryo. We may take the example of the world of science. In a scientific congress there are no more barriers, everyone lives in the same thought, a scientist works for the community, and the work is increasingly team work. We could equally well take the example of religions, since a properly understood religion is a link uniting all men in a spirit which transcends racial oppositions.

At this point it is essential to cite the admirable reflections of François Russo: "Socialization is by no means a superficial and purely sociological phenomenon. It concerns the essential destiny of mankind. It constitutes a fundamental 'drive' of mankind, compared with which wars and cultural transformations are purely secondary things. Socialization appears as *a prolongation of biological evolution*, but in another mode. Far from diminishing beings, socialization enriches them and liberates them. It contributes to the affirmation and blossoming of the person. Socialization marks the beginning of the era of the person. More essentially, it is the manifestation, on the scale no longer purely of the couple or of the family, but of Mankind and of the Universe, of *union in love*. (. . .).

The great merit of Father Teilhard's conception of socialization is to underline the *significance* of socialization which, even today, is still too much regarded as a simple fact to which Christianity must merely adjust itself, as a situation which merely has to be adjusted so that the person is not crushed by numbers, but which raises no essential problems."[1]

[1] Seminar on Teilhard de Chardin, Venice, 11 June 1962, *Socialization*.

PHASE V: THE DISTANT FUTURE: This is constituted by the complete emergence of that planetized mankind. What is the point to which the history of the universe is tending? To interiorize this unification, men must be ready to unite, there must be a focus of evolution, point Omega. What are the properties of Omega? The focus of evolution is first of all spiritual, since, in order to move a spiritual being, there must be a spiritual focus. The focus must be eternal, since nature become conscious cannot agree to go to its destruction. This focus must be an immanent focus, it must be internal to man. It must, moreover, be a personal focus, since it is hard to see why evolution should have been at such pains to elaborate the human person if it were destined to be abolished. And to justify the vital impulse of humanity, this person must be a transcendent person, a person who outstrips man, who must be situated *on another level*. In fact, if we try to make a concrete, existential analysis of man, we feel that humanity is not sufficient for him, that it is a focus too similar to himself, that man is in perpetual suspense, and that the only thing which can move him is a transcendent person. Finally, the focus must be a focus of charity, of love. It therefore clearly constitutes a point of emergence and achievement.

Naturally, it is impossible to *predict* a new unprecedented emergence, precisely because it is a new creation. This is what constitutes the surprise and beauty of this effort, which always breathes a charm, the charm of the extraordinary.

Thus, as François Russo sums it up, "The movement of socialization is leading mankind towards a 'critical point', a 'super-state of psychic tension', a 'higher pole of consciousness', where a 'way out' becomes manifest, the only possible way out for Mankind. Thus a 'reversion into the Other' becomes operative, a passage to 'another face of the Universe'. Thus an 'ultra-humanization' is effected, thus an 'ultra-human' becomes manifest. Mankind attains a 'second critical point of reflection', a 'critical point of socialization'. But since this 'ultra-revolution' is now taking place in a reflecting environment, it can only be a self-evolution, that is to say '*a consciously and passionately willed act*'."[1]

... Let us take stock: (1) It is evident that, in discussing this fifth phase we have encroached on the "dialectic", since on the plane of a scientific phenomenology, the point Omega remains "of a conjectural and postulated character"; (2) the passage between the higher pole of

[1] Russo, *op. cit.*

consciousness and Christ Omega presupposes a reversion and a point of annihilation. There is therefore no confusion between the "natural" and the "supernatural" planes.

Teilhard's method of thought is therefore very strict and very original. It is not a positive science in the technical sense of the word, but it is genuinely science, a unitary science, generalized and extrapolated because of the search for meaning, in short an ideal regulator for scientific research. It is not a myth, in the sense of *Timaeus*, since myth, by means of fabulation, seeks to describe a zone which partly escapes pure ideas (the only true object of science and philosophy according to Plato), whether this zone is contaminated by the existential or by the sensible. It is not metaphysics, a deductive approach starting from abstract principles. Neither is it theology, although this thought leads to theology. It is a phenomenology with a very new aspect, which presents itself as universal history, which is perhaps the best way to philosophize. It is, even better, a dialectic of nature in Engels' sense, although Teilhard cannot be said to have traversed Marxism, or to have baptized or surmounted it.

In reading THE PHENOMENON OF MAN, Marxists have not been mistaken. Roger Garaudy once said to the author something like this: "If Engels, at the end of the nineteenth century, had had all the scientific data, and especially the palaeontological and anthropological data, available to Teilhard, he would have written something comparable to THE PHENOMENON OF MAN, less the religious part."

Thus, Teilhard, in surmounting anguish, went beyond existentialism. In elaborating *his* dialectic of nature, he has gone beyond Marxism. His power of synthesis has enabled him to dominate the two great streams of contemporary thought, which he absorbs and synthesizes.

In more precise fashion, Teilhard has demonstrated that time is intelligible, since this time, while remaining the natural dimension of divine creation, and therefore the vehicle of emergence, obeys a dialectic and represents a convergent environment. *Time is convergent*, that is Teilhard's major contribution to the major problem of modern thought, time.

IV   CHRISTOLOGY[1]

THE PHENOMENON OF MAN is not a theology, but may serve as a Propylaea to theology. In effect, there is theology in Teilhard, but this theology is, as it were, in suspension in his whole thought, which makes it hard to discover. The well-known problems of the theologian are to be found in Teilhard, but Teilhard throws the specialists off their stride, because these problems are not presented under the envelope or in the categories proper to this order of research, theology being a science which has its own problematics, its own technicalities. This is what creates the interest of Teilhard's thought. The theology of a theologian bears its own subject and its own limits, whence the interest of the dialogue between the theologian and the non-theologian. But, with Teilhard, the dialogue is internal to his project. It is not exactly a dialogue between a theologian and a non-theologian, but it is a conversation between self and self in the framework of a single overall vision of the whole, the theology remaining closely attached to this thought and not to be dissociated from it. This is the reproach which the theologians have levelled against Teilhard.

What, then, is this theological thought of Teilhard's? It is completely centred on Christ. Teilhard always has a Christology in view. His thought elaborates materials which allow the themes of Christology to be taken up in the course of an overall vision assuming the totality of the intelligible world. Two problems can be distinguished; Christ is God-man, and therefore the presence of God in man takes place at a determined time in history. Hence a first question: what is the value of this determined time when it is given its place in overall time? All theologians are agreed in making Christological time the key of total time, but this agreement masks divergences in the concept of time. Another point: Christ presents himself as the being in whom everything which exists finds its meaning. Hence a second question: how can this Christ present himself as the meaning and secret of the totality of the knowable or the real?

These two questions have been given a series of different answers, sometimes in fairly diverse directions. One of their common features is that the theologians have never been able to escape the examination of the relation between what they construct in the framework of

[1] We merely summarize and adapt an admirable talk by Pastor Georges Crespy to the Catholic Centre of French Intellectuals, on 18 February 1962.

Christology and what is given in the framework of our knowledge of the world. Thus, we find ourselves faced with a twofold task, to specify the temporal significance of Christ for the temporal totality, and to define the relation between the Christic happening and cosmology.

Now, on these two problems, Teilhard's thought makes a considerable contribution, which is irreversible (which does not mean that it cannot be revised)—irreversible in the sense that it is henceforth impossible to go back on it. As we have said, it is not as a theologian, in the strict sense, that Teilhard brings us this material, since it is important to refer, in the first place, to his overall problematics. The intuition which strikes Teilhard is that the totality of objects is organized along an axis, time, the framework within which phenomena unfold. But this framework is not a neutral and indifferent receptacle, it is oriented, polarized, like a vector or a certain type of light. Within this time, reality organizes itself, it tends towards its maximum. Not only are we in the presence of a temporal framework, but this framework orders the dynamic force which governs the development of every kind of phenomenon, of the overall evolution of the cosmos.

The great problem is the term of this evolution (for if evolution were random and amorphous there would be no reason to take it seriously).

As soon as it becomes a question of evolution, we therefore have the choice between two general lines of approach, since we can comprehend an evolution either by its commencement or by its term; this second method being much more forward-looking, and enabling us to seize characteristics which would otherwise escape us. In appearance, we must therefore choose between a point Alpha (the initial) and Omega (the terminal). But if we had to choose in reality, our vision would be feeble. For example, a point Omega which did not proceed from a point Alpha would be in danger of appearing purely contingent. There must be something already recognizable, pre-existent or pre-emerged.

Now Teilhard makes use of a sound method, the method of recurrence. We have already said that evolution is a recurrent growth, that is to say that it passes through phases which repeat themselves at different levels and in different fashions. That is not the question here. For Teilhard, this point Omega is not only the contingent or necessary conclusion of a process, it should appear as a means of signification for the whole evolution which runs up to it, a retrospective flash which results in the affirmation of a point Alpha, that point Alpha which Christian thought demands in order to avoid falling into the pantheism of the God-who-makes-himself. Now, between Alpha and Omega, there is a tension, and there must be a whole series of exchanges. It is here that Teilhard's thought contributes a decisive element.

In effect, at this point Omega of the natural convergence of social-ized mankind, we also find Christ Omega. By the cosmic Christ, or universal Christ, or Christ Omega, Teilhard introduces the Christo-logical categories which the theologians had separated from the cos-mological categories. Christology will play, with Teilhard, the role of a reality imposing a meaning on the cosmos, the role of a revealing reality. It is this Christology which gives his whole adventure all its significance. Amputated of its Christology, Teilhard's effort loses a great part of its meaning and nothing remains but a plausible pheno-menology. The appearance of a Christology will consolidate the whole of Teilhard's adventure. From point Omega Christ becomes the whole meaning of this evolution, he becomes the whole axis of this evolution of the world.

The study of this parousiac point is decisive for an understanding of Teilhard. Generally courses in Christology start by tackling the theme of the pre-existence of Christ, and analyse the very rich concept of the Word; what is this Logos of which John speaks? They then go on to speak of the birth of this Logos, and then to deal with Christ's royal, prophetic ministry, ending with an excursus towards the Parousia, examining the various theses on the probable end of the world, those unfounded assumptions which are the children of our ignorance. But the major difficulty is not tackled; how can we reconcile this internal movement of Christology with the whole movement of the world? Now, Teilhard enables us better to envisage this fundamental problem. Starting from Omega, and descending by recurrence, by a sort of return shock in the direction of Alpha, Christology recovers a new coherence and becomes synthesized with a cosmology founded on the concept of nature. Teilhard makes it possible to adopt a projected cosmology which takes its whole meaning from this projected Christol-ogy, since the world is not a reality virtually separated from its Creator.

In sum, his Christological perspective enables Teilhard to unfold a vision of time which, in the traditional Christology, is not always coherent. In the New Testament we find propositions on time which are not always easy to reconcile: (1) the time was fulfilled, this was the moment when God sent his Son; (2) all possible times take their meaning from the history of Jesus; (3) beyond the Resurrection time continues, but its meaning is only comprehensible in relation to a twofold event, the Resurrection and the Parousia. In sum, we are witnessing a flattening of the time of human history. Basically, we find in the New Testament no reflection on duration, except perhaps the category of imminence. For the authors of the New Testament, it is the Kerygma, it is the coming of the Good News, which will colour all history to come, a whole will be defined in relation to this event. For example, in the Apocalypse, all the events are presented in the framework of a confrontation between what pertains to Christ and what does not, the fundamental category being the victory of Christ.

But it is difficult for this category to live once it has been learned that the world is in evolution. In practice, eschatological impatience conflicts with the infinite patience of time in producing what is ultimately produced. For the New Testament, human historical time is time in which nothing much seems to happen, I mean between death and resurrection on the one hand and the Parousia on the other. For science, time is a time in which something is always happening, a time, if I may use the phrase, which has time to spare. Thus, if it is to remain faithful to the Kerygma, our spirit is torn. On the one hand, I await with impatience the return of Christ; on the other hand, when I talk about science, I am thinking in terms of hundreds of centuries. In the face of this situation something must be introduced to reconcile the hour-glass time of the world with the time which is revealing for all time. Now Teilhard proposes that we should understand and live time for the use of cosmology as a Christic time, within which Christ is present as the animating element; Christ is there as one who inserts himself in history, in the very heart of history, one who will super-animate it and take charge of it.

Obviously, Teilhard's thought is disconcerting for us. Can this Christ who lived in a Mediterranean world super-animate the evolution of the whole world? Can the Jesus adored by our piety, who lived in Palestine, become without difficulty and without problem the Christ who is the animator of evolution? There is, of course, the traditional solution. Everyone agrees in thinking that Christ lives in his church, in the sacraments, in the preaching of the word. It is a presence which can, as it were, be labelled. As for the non-Christians, Christ is present just the same, though the mode of his presence remains mysterious. This is what might be called the ecclesiastical solution, reached at the conclusion of a labour of separation which perhaps amputates the total Christ of a great part of his being and his meaning.

We therefore remain somewhat unsatisfied. How can Christ present among his own be given all his meaning? Teilhard answers, by the perpetual reincorporation of the Christian phylum in the history of the world, by an effort to think Christ on the scale of the whole world. From then on, the presence of Christ takes on the aspect of a total presence in which the ecclesiastical presence rediscovers all its meaning. Henceforth, to be Christians, we must throw ourselves open with this Christ to the totality of a world which belongs to him by its structure and by its purpose, since Christ is Omega, the aim of the universe. Teilhard takes up and enlarges a Pauline vein, for St. Paul, in some magnificent passages, shows us God recapitulating everything in Christ, the head and consummator of all things. A pressing question then arises: could not this theological vein be taken up again?

One criticism remains possible. It may be objected that it is not certain that St. Paul's thought on Christ Pantokrator, the master of all things, can be adjusted to Teilhard's thought. There are several arts of being Pauline. With St. Paul, the representation of Christ glorious is closely related to the vision of Christ on the cross; it is because of his abasement that he will receive the kingdom and the power. Behind the Pauline thought we can discover a tragic perspective, and this Greek category of the tragic helps us to understand the enlightenment of St. Paul. With him, the decisive factor is the Christ who had to win a victory over death, the fruit of sin. Pauline thought unfolds against a relatively catastrophic background of sin and death, the liberty of man being menaced by this presence of evil. Now, on a superficial examination, we might be astonished not to find this presence of evil in Teilhard. A Christology without the dying Christ is incomplete. And we could continue these reservations by adding that the problematics of evil is surprising in Teilhard, who makes evil a by-product of this advance of the world, evil belonging to the order of evolution and not being a radically alien element.

This, then, is a difficulty. It does not seem to us to be insurmountable. We might first recall the concepts of St. Augustine, making evil an inevitable obverse. In practice, being, having been created *ex nihilo*, extracted from nothing, participates both of the plenitude of God and of nothingness. But this reference to St. Augustine was not strictly indispensable. We have said enough of anguish in Teilhard. An optimism which relegates the cross to the background is far from being the last word of Teilhard's theological thought. Teilhard lived too close to the suffering Christ. It is true that Teilhard regards the problem of evil as theoretically solved. But why? The problem of evil is not theoretically solved in the sense that evil is inevitable and that we shall benefit from a continuous growth of good—on this last point, moreover, Teilhard has said exactly the opposite, since he thinks that the temptation to revolt will grow with the progress of reflecting consciousness. No, but for Teilhard the problem of evil is solved by the very presence of Christ. Evil is there with all its horrors, but the last word lies with the One who succeeds in incorporating evil in his project itself, namely Christ. Teilhard's optimism is based on the certitude that it is in Christ that the problem of evil finds its solution. Teilhard does not present the tragic, as being absorbed by speculative means, he presents the evil as overcome by Christ, who takes command of evil and suffering. This is not a solution along the lines of Leibniz on the completion of a rational research, or in other words, a theodicy. Teilhard helps us to put the question properly, for it is putting it wrongly to postulate first what is evil and then what is Christ. For Teilhard the sequence must be inverted, the plenitude of Christ must be affirmed first, and then the problem of evil must be posed. Thus there is no longer any danger of hurling ourselves into unbelief by postulating either a God who is good but powerless, or a God who is powerful but not good.

Thus this Christology of Teilhard enables us to take up and reconstruct a great many Christological themes. It further enables us to relax the tension between the theological themes and the cosmological themes. Teilhard's interest is therefore virtually inexhaustible. Teilhard helps us again to make our own a projected unity of mind. With him it is not necessary to turn alternately to the theologian and the scientist. What is essential is to start precisely from a projected unity of mind and to set the theological themes and the scientific themes in relation to this frame of reference. When the theologian is tempted by pride, and believes that he has a solution for every kind of intellectual problem, then the scientist rises up, which creates an untenable situation of false dialogue. Teilhard, for his part, has presented a possibility of coalescence between Christ and the world, between theological reflection and scientific reflection. He gives us the hope that these divisions can still be overcome. Naturally, they can never be overcome in their entirety. As men, we shall never attain to the fullness of knowledge, but we must make its promise actual. Teilhard is a keystone in this total knowledge. To organize my reflections around this determination of humble expectation is far more fruitful than allowing them to be resigned to this unbearable division of knowledge, a compartmentalization which, if it were carried to the extreme, would result in a sort of schizophrenia. Teilhard assembles together all men who desire to live out this projected unity of knowledge actively and joyously. The Lord Jesus will come quickly only if we expect him greatly. Teilhard's theological thought, which is human and therefore imperfect, is open to correction. But the whole question is whether or not we start from Teilhard, whether we are prepared to allow ourselves to be led by Teilhard's thought to the frontiers of this total vision. All those who have revolted against the fact that Christ is not recognized in his total dimensions thank God for the gift to Christians of Pierre Teilhard de Chardin.

THE ASSOCIATION

There is a growing awareness of the relevance and importance of Teilhard's thought all over the world. Many social topics of the greatest significance are discussed by him in the context of scientific analyses of the evolutionary process. The implications of his theories are very far-reaching for the future of man. They need to be studied and discussed in relation to every aspect of human society.

The Association is an educational organisation whose activities include:

Organising study groups throughout Great Britain and Ireland
Arranging meetings, conferences and symposia
Setting up a central library and archives
Providing an information service to all enquirers
Publishing twice yearly THE TEILHARD REVIEW—free to members
Promoting films, television and radio broadcasts
Promoting the publication of a study series THE TEILHARD STUDY LIBRARY
Maintaining contacts with Associations in other countries pursuing similar aims
Encouraging the growth of affiliated Associations in the Commonwealth

To further these activities the Association must rely on voluntary donations, especially through the subscription of members, where possible by Deed of Covenant. You are invited to assist the Association's work through membership and participation in its activities. Minimum subscriptions are:

Ordinary Members	Two guineas per annum
Group Members	Five guineas per annum
Student Members	One guinea per annum

THE PIERRE TEILHARD DE CHARDIN ASSOCIATION
OF GREAT BRITAIN AND IRELAND

3 Cromwell Place, London S.W.7   (Telephone 01.584 7734)

INDEX OF NAMES

Numbers in italics refer to footnotes

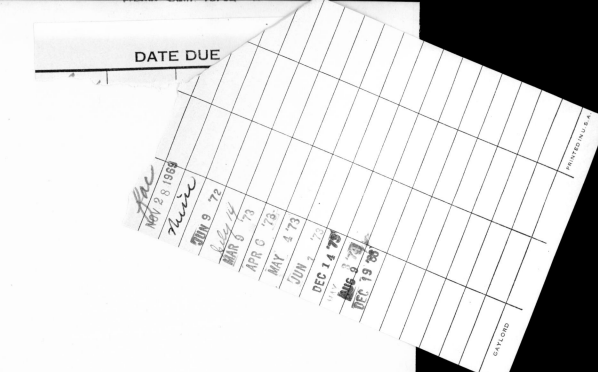